Planning Permission Made Easy

A Homeowner's Guide

Alan Gunne-Jones BA (Hons) MRTPI FCMI FRGS

RICS

Published by the Royal Institution of Chartered Surveyors
Surveyor Court
Westwood Business Park
Coventry CV4 8JE
UK
www.ricsbooks.com

No responsibility for loss or damage caused to any person acting or refraining from action as a result of the material included in this publication can be accepted by the author or RICS.

ISBN 978 1 84219 447 8

© Royal Institution of Chartered Surveyors (RICS) April 2009. Copyright in all or part of this publication rests with RICS, and save by prior consent of RICS, no part or parts shall be reproduced by any means electronic, mechanical, photocopying or otherwise, now known or to be devised.

Typeset in Great Britain by Columns Design Ltd, Reading, Berks

Printed by Page Bros, Norwich

Mixed Sources
Product group from well-managed forests, and other controlled sources
www.fsc.org Cert no. TT-COC-002706
© 1996 Forest Stewardship Council
FSC

Contents

Preface vii
About the author ix
Acknowledgments xi

1	Introduction	1
2	The planning system	4
3	Frequently asked questions	12
	What is development?	12
	What is Permitted Development?	13
	What is a development plan?	14
	What is a dwelling?	16
	What is the 'original building'?	18
	What is the curtilage of a dwelling?	18
	What are 'purposes incidental' to the enjoyment of a dwelling?	19
	What are the Use Classes?	20
	What is a highway?	20
	What is a listed building?	21
	What is a conservation area?	22
	What is a Scheduled Ancient Monument?	24
	Who is my local planning authority?	24

Contents

	What is Article 1(5) land?	26
	What is an advertisement?	27
	What is an Area of Special Control of Advertisements?	29
	What is an Environmental Impact Assessment?	29
	What is a Tree Preservation Order?	31
	Who can apply for planning permission?	32
	What happens if I live in Scotland, Wales or Northern Ireland?	32
	Will I need assistance?	33
	Will I need any other consents or approvals?	35
4	Measurements, dimensions and drawings	43
5	What can I do without permission – in my home?	47
6	What can I do without permission – in my garden?	62
7	I don't need planning permission – great! What do I do next?	73
8	So I need permission – what now?	93
9	They said no! – what do I do?	121
10	Why don't I just start work without planning permission?	139
11	How do I stop neighbouring developments?	144

List of local planning authorities in England and Wales	155
Where can I find more information?	192
Glossary	195
Abbreviations	206
Standard householder planning application form	207

Contents

Householder planning application and conservation area consent form   213

Householder planning application and listed building consent form   219

Planning appeal form   226

Enforcement notice appeal form   234

Index   241

Preface

We are a nation of DIY enthusiasts. The Office for National Statistics (ONS) reveals that the average British man spends 25 minutes a day on DIY and home repairs. Between 1996 and 2006, our spending on DIY products increased by 76 per cent, in 'real' terms, i.e. taking into account the rise in prices. In comparison, during the same period we spent 10 per cent less on the services of tradesmen – electricians, plumbers, carpenters, and so on. With the increased costs of moving home and people deciding to stay put in order to maintain access to good schools, doctors and dentists, as well as a growing tendency for our adult children to stay in the family home, or to return to live with us after completing their education, the pressure to extend or adapt our homes is intense. According to the ONS, from 1991 to 2006, there was an eight per cent increase in children in their early twenties living at home with their parents. These are the KIPPERS – 'kids in parents pockets eroding retirement saving'. Falling house prices provide further incentive for people to stay put rather than move on and, consequently, more and more of us are likely to turn our attention to home improvements.

The book is therefore aimed at *homeowners* who, for one or other of these reasons, are faced with the challenge of improving their homes. Home improvements come in a variety of forms – including extensions, conservatories, carports, decking, sheds and swimming pools, etc. – and

Preface

are carried out at the home or in the garden. Most require permission in some form or another, e.g. Building Regulations approval, Landlord Consent or planning permission, although an increasing number are now exempt from the latter. Planning permission is, however, one of the most complicated approval processes you are likely to encounter.

Many home improvements are minor in scale, but they dominate the planning system. Approximately half of all planning applications in England concern domestic building work. If you have ever sat through a meeting of your local council's planning committee, you will have observed how contentious and emotive the issue of 'developments' by homeowners can be, particularly where they have given rise to objections from neighbours.

Although recent announcements by the UK government have increased the range of home improvements that can be undertaken without planning permission, this will not take the emotion or complexity out of the process. There will still be complaints from neighbours and increased pressure on councils to investigate even when the building work does not require planning permission. And there will also be pressure to ensure that any additional consents or approvals have been obtained.

The aim of this book is to provide advice and guidance to help you ensure that the home improvements you are proposing – and those of your neighbours – are legal, but most importantly that they do not adversely impact the enjoyment of your home and garden.

Planning is a constantly changing system, but the rules and regulations contained in this book were correct at the time of going to press.

Alan Gunne-Jones BA (Hons) MRTPI FCMI FRGS

December 2008

About the author

Alan Gunne-Jones BA (Hons) MRTPI FCMI FRGS is a chartered town planner with extensive experience of planning in both the private and public sectors in the UK and overseas.

He is a Director of Tribal MJP, a planning and development consultancy with offices in London, Bristol and Kent.

Alan is author of *Planning – Is It a Service and How Can it Be Effective?*, which was commissioned by the Royal Town Planning Institute, and *Town Planning – A Practical Guide*, published by RICS in 2009. He is a regular contributor to the technical press, including the *Watts Pocket Handbook,* published annually by RICS, and also provides the town planning compliance section for RICS *isurv building surveying* (www.isurvlive.co.uk). Alan sits on the editorial board of the RICS *isurv planning* (www.isurv.comwww.isurv.com).

Acknowledgments

I am particularly grateful to the Editorial Board of RICS for providing the opportunity to write this book, which I felt, was badly needed to simplify an increasingly complex aspect of our current planning system.

I would like to acknowledge the very important part played by RICS Commissioning Editor Emma Harris, who was not only instrumental in bringing the book to fruition, but also initiated the idea of the book in the first place. I am also indebted to Jan Bowmer, who copy-edited the book with such diligence.

Finally, I wish to thank my wife and family for their suggestions, research, ideas and proofreading contributions, but most of all for their patience and overriding support without which the book would not have been published.

1 Introduction

With the cost of moving house averaging £16,000, it's not surprising that more and more homeowners are resorting to improving their existing accommodation, either by making internal alterations or adding extensions. Moreover, in light of the current state of the housing market, many people are choosing to stay in their current home and improve what they have.

The Sunday Times Home section recently identified its top ten tips for adding value to your home:

- install an ensuite bathroom;
- convert the loft;
- extend the kitchen;
- convert the garage;
- put in a skylight;
- add a utility room;
- paint the front door and woodwork;
- renovate the floorboards;
- landscape the garden; and
- open up the fireplace.

(Maslen, C., *Improve to move*, article in *Home* section, *The Sunday Times*, London, February 2009.)

INTRODUCTION

Many of these works will require planning permission. In 2007, nearly half of all planning applications in England were for minor alterations in the form of extensions, porches, fences, gates and walls and satellite dishes, etc., and since 1997 the number of such applications has doubled.

All of this means that homeowners are increasingly coming into contact with the planning system, either through their aspirations to improve their own property or because of their neighbours' ambitions to do likewise. For this reason, this guide is specifically aimed at homeowners – whether freeholders or leaseholders – and seeks to demystify the planning process by explaining what changes you are allowed to make without planning permission – and which ones you can't. And, in the event that you *do* require planning permission, you will discover what you need to do to put in an application as well as what action to take should permission be refused. You will also find guidance on how to monitor and influence the planning process to ensure that your neighbours do not undertake any home improvements that could detract from the amenity and enjoyment of your own home.

The term 'homeowner' is used throughout this book and it covers owners, leaseholders and tenants. Regardless of your legal status, you may be considering improvement works to your home, although if you are a leaseholder you may have to obtain consent from the freeholder before doing so or, if a tenant, from your landlord. The planning system uses the term 'householder' rather than 'homeowner' to represent proposals for domestic building work. So, throughout the planning system, the relatively minor category of works that homeowners may be contemplating are commonly referred to as 'householder applications'.

In planning, the term 'dwelling' or 'dwellinghouse' is used in its widest sense to include houses, bungalows and

ACKNOWLEDGMENTS

flats, although there is an important distinction between dwellings and flats which limits the scope of home improvements that flat owners are allowed to undertake without planning permission. Throughout this book, though, the term 'home' or 'house' refers to a dwelling or a flat.

So, in short, if you are a homeowner who is proposing to undertake any building work at your house or in your garden, you'll find advice on whether you can carry out the work without planning permission. And, should you require permission, you'll discover how to go about obtaining it and what to do if it's denied.

⚠ Flats, and buildings containing flats, are subject to greater planning constraints than dwellings

⇨ What is a dwelling? **page 16**

⇨ Will your works require planning permission? **chapters 5 and 6**

⇨ How to prepare and submit a planning application **chapter 8**

⇨ What to do if planning permission is refused **chapter 9**

2 The planning system

The planning system has been in place since 1947 and its primary purpose is to regulate the use of land in the public interest. Essentially, the system is designed to control development (which can include home improvements or building works) through a process that requires anyone wishing to carry out such works to apply for permission to do so. Applications for planning permission are submitted to and considered by the relevant local planning authority. For ease of reference throughout this book, the local planning authority is referred to as the 'local council' or 'your council'.

⇨ Who is my local planning authority? **page 24**

The key planning acts

For the homeowner the legal basis for the planning system is provided by the following acts:

- *Town and Country Planning Act* 1990;
- *Planning (Listed Buildings and Conservation Areas) Act* 1990;
- *Planning and Compensation Act* 1991;
- *Planning and Compulsory Purchase Act* 2004; and the
- *Planning Act* 2008.

The most relevant of these acts for homeowners will be the *Town and Country Planning Act* 1990, which defines 'development' and the process by which development proposals are assessed and determined. Throughout the book, this is referred to as the '1990 Act'.

The most recent Act – the 2008 Planning Act – has introduced powers that allow:

- the right for the Planning Inspectorate (a government body appointed by the secretary of state to deal with appeals) to determine the method by which appeals should be progressed;
- the introduction of a charge for appeals; and
- the right for councils to accept minor amendments to planning permissions without the need for a fresh planning application.

At the time of going to press, these powers had not been brought into effect.

The key test for all development

The primary test for determining if individual development proposals are acceptable is set out in the 1990 Act and further strengthened in section 38(6) of the 2004 Act which requires that:

> '... if regard is to be had to the development plan for the purpose of any determination to be made under the planning Acts the determination must be made in accordance with the plan unless material considerations indicate otherwise.'

In practice, this means that your development project will be assessed against the policies contained in the development plan for your area. If it is found to be in conflict with these policies, then you will need to provide justification as to why planning permission should be granted.

⇨ What is a development plan? **page 14**

Permitted Development rights

Some types of development are allowed by a Development Order issued by the government and therefore do not require a planning application to be made to the council. These Permitted Development rights were introduced under secondary legislation to allow householders, in particular, freedom to undertake some home improvements without the need to obtain planning permission. In October 2008, the rights were extended to cover a wider range of building projects and these changes are estimated to remove approximately 80,000 planning applications from the planning system each year.

The main Development Orders that affect homeowners are the:

- *Town and Country Planning (General Permitted Development) Order* 1995 (SI No. 418);

- *Town and Country Planning (General Permitted Development) (Amendment) Order* 1998 (SI No. 462);

- *Town and Country Planning (General Permitted Development) (Amendment) (England) Order* 2008 (SI No. 675); and the

- *Town and Country Planning (General Permitted Development) (Amendment) (No. 2) (England) Order* 2008 (SI No. 2362).

Collectively, these are referred throughout this book as the 'planning regulations'.

Local Development Plans and Regional Spatial Strategies

As well as the development control process, the future needs of the community have to be considered and this is done through the preparation of Local Development Plans.

LOCAL DEVELOPMENT PLANS

Each council has a responsibility to prepare a development plan for its area that sets out how the area is to be developed or safeguarded in the future. Plans can be prepared for the whole council area or for specific settlements or sub-areas. Councils are also obligated to keep their development plans under review and bring forward proposals to update them on a regular basis.

In addition to the Local Development Plan, there is a regional level of development planning which outlines the overall strategy for each region in terms of housing, employment, transport, infrastructure, etc., and targets for these are contained within individual Regional Spatial Strategies (RSSs). If you are a homeowner who is planning to carry out domestic building works, RSSs will be of lesser interest to you than the Local Development Plan. But, for the purposes of the planning system, the overall development plan for a region is represented by both the RSS and the individual development plans. In the case of Greater London, the regional planning policy is provided within the London Plan and, although this is equivalent to a RSS, it does contain some policies that may be of relevance to homeowner proposals.

Generally, the development plans for individual districts or boroughs will be of much greater significance for homeowners because these can impact individual properties or surrounding areas. Over the past few years, the development plan system has been in transition. It is moving from a system based on Regional Policy Guidance notes (RPGs), county structure and district local plans and borough Unitary Development Plans (UDPs) to Regional Spatial Strategies (RSSs) and Local Development Frameworks (LDFs). The existing county structure plans will soon disappear and the role of county councils will eventually be limited to developments involving waste and minerals only.

⇨ More about Local Development Plans **page 14**

Local Development Frameworks

The new system of LDFs is designed to offer greater flexibility to both councils and planners because it consists of a series of policy documents that can be individually prepared and reviewed without requiring the whole development plan to be considered. The LDF will eventually comprise a core strategy, a statement of community involvement and then a collection of individual development documents, such as site allocations; affordable housing and housing policy, and suchlike. Since most councils are currently working on the preparation of their LDFs, you may already be involved in or aware of local consultations taking place and therefore familiar with the ever increasing use of acronyms such as SDPs (supplementary planning documents), LDDs (Local Development Documents), and so on, which might seem perplexing at first, but are a feature of the Local Development Framework process.

When looking at individual planning applications, councils are required to consider how the proposal fits in with the Local Development Plan and must make their decisions in accordance with this plan unless there are material considerations that dictate otherwise. Material considerations could include new statements of government policy, emerging planning policy and generally anything that relates to the use and development of land.

National planning policy guidance

Over the years, the government has issued a number of policy statements concerning various aspects of planning and development. These are known as Planning Policy Guidance notes (PPGs) or Planning Policy Statements (PPSs). The latter are gradually replacing PPGs and provide a more succinct statement of planning policy. For homeowners, the most relevant of these is the Planning

Policy Statement PPS1 on 'Delivering sustainable development', which was published in January 2005 and sets out the government's overall objectives for the planning system and the national planning policies that should be applied in preparing development plans and taking decisions on individual planning applications.

The government also issues a number of circulars on more detailed aspects of the planning system. If you are a homeowner, most of these will be of no interest to you, although some of them will be relevant and, in such cases, you will have to familiarise yourself with their contents. Each circular is prefixed by a number and year for reference. For example, Circular 01/2006 provides guidance on changes to the development control system and, in particular, the purpose and objectives of Design and Access Statements. The latter are intended to encourage you to think about how your proposal fits onto the site and into the local area and how it might affect others, for instance the impact on your neighbours. In addition, the statement should include an explanation of how access will be provided both to and within the site for different groups of people. When applying for planning permission for any proposed works, you may be required to attach these statements to your planning application.

⇨ More on Design and Access Statements **page 102**

The structure of the planning system

The overall structure of the planning system is represented in the following figure.

THE PLANNING SYSTEM

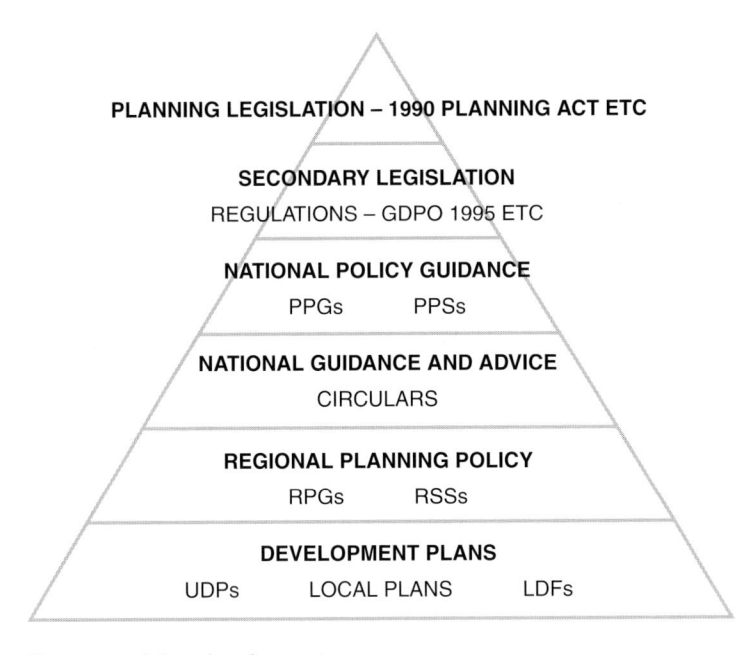

```
              PLANNING LEGISLATION – 1990 PLANNING ACT ETC

                      SECONDARY LEGISLATION
                     REGULATIONS – GDPO 1995 ETC

                      NATIONAL POLICY GUIDANCE
                         PPGs      PPSs

                    NATIONAL GUIDANCE AND ADVICE
                             CIRCULARS

                      REGIONAL PLANNING POLICY
                         RPGs      RSSs

                        DEVELOPMENT PLANS
                  UDPs      LOCAL PLANS      LDFs
```

Structure of the planning system

Right of appeal

If you have made a planning application to the council and the outcome is unsatisfactory, then you have a right of appeal to the secretary of state. The right of appeal extends to applications that have been refused permission, or where the council has given permission but imposed conditions that are onerous or unacceptable, or if the council has failed to deal with an application within a statutory defined time period. The statutory time period for minor applications – and almost all applications submitted by homeowners are categorised as minor – is eight weeks. Appeals are heard and decided on by independent inspectors who work for the Planning Inspectorate, the government agency set up to administer the appeals process.

⇨   More on planning appeals **chapter 9**

Summary

So, the critical question for you as a homeowner is whether the development works you are considering can be carried out without planning permission. Unless the work is already permitted by a Development Order promoted by the government, you must apply to your local council for planning permission. First, though, you will need to understand some of the key terms and phrases that are commonplace in planning. Once you are familiar with these, you will find it easier to manoeuvre your way through the maze of the planning system.

The planning system – some key facts
- The *Town And Country Planning Act* 1990 provides the main legal basis for the planning system.
- If you want to carry out home improvements that will affect the exterior of your home, you may have to apply for planning permission.
- Some home improvements can be carried out without the need for planning permission under the Permitted Development rights.
- Applications for planning permission are made to your local district or borough council.
- Your local council is responsible for preparing the development plan for the future of your area.
- The council will determine planning applications in accordance with the Local Development Plan unless material considerations dictate otherwise.
- The government provides guidelines on various aspects of planning in the form of guidance notes, statements and circulars and councils must take these into consideration when determining planning applications.
- If your planning application is refused, you have a right of appeal to the secretary of state.

3 Frequently asked questions

Once you start to get involved in the planning process, you'll have to get to grips with some of the key terms used. It's important to understand how the planning system defines words such as 'development', 'dwelling', 'homeowner', etc., and to familiarise yourself with some of the other regulations and controls that often work in tandem with the planning process.

This chapter explains some of the more commonly used terms and phrases and provides a starting point for your journey into the planning system. You will also find a glossary at the back of the book.

What is development?

One of the primary functions of the planning system is to regulate development activity. In improving, extending or altering your home and garden you will undoubtedly be undertaking some form of building work. But first you need to know whether what you want to do actually falls under the definition of development and, if it does, whether you will require planning permission.

Development is clearly defined in the 1990 Act as:

> '. . . the carrying out of building, engineering, mining or other operations in, on, over or under land, or the making of any material change in the use of any buildings or other land.'

The 1990 Act confirms that the carrying out of works for the maintenance, improvement or other alteration of any building that affect only the interior of a building or which do not materially affect the external appearance of the building *is not* development. Similarly, the use of any buildings or other land within your garden, or what is referred to as the curtilage of a dwellinghouse, for any purpose that is incidental to the enjoyment of that dwellinghouse *is not* development. Planning permission is therefore not required for works within your home or for works that do not materially affect the outside of the house. So any works involving, for example, the conversion of two rooms into one or the opening up of a room will not require planning permission, although if they include any structural works, then Building Regulations approval may be needed.

To avoid any doubt, the use as two or more separate dwellinghouses of any building previously used as a single dwellinghouse involves a material change of use and, therefore, planning permission will be required to convert your home into flats.

⇨ What is the curtilage of a dwelling? **page 18**

⇨ More about Building Regulations approval **page 77**

What is Permitted Development?

It may be that the type of development you are proposing is already permitted as a result of changes to the planning laws in recent years and this can save you the time and expense of applying for planning permission.

Permitted Development is development that is already allowed under an order or regulation issued by the government. The building works would ordinarily require planning permission, but, because of the minor nature of such works, the government has in effect already

FREQUENTLY ASKED QUESTIONS

approved them and so there's no need for a planning application to be submitted to the council. Permitted Development rights are quite extensive and apply to homeowners, statutory and other organisations and public authorities. They are usually granted subject to conditions and do not apply in all areas. In some particularly sensitive areas, e.g. conservation areas, National Parks and Areas of Outstanding Natural Beauty, the extent of Permitted Development rights is more limited.

As a homeowner you have quite a wide range of Permitted Development rights that allow you to extend or alter your home and garden. However, these rights are subject to various conditions and caveats and you will need to study the 'fine print' before you embark on your building project. You will find more information about the range of building works you are entitled to carry out in chapters 5 and 6.

⚠ Conservation areas, National Parks and Areas of Outstanding Natural Beauty are subject to greater restraints on Permitted Development rights

⚠ Don't assume all your works will be covered under Permitted Development – check if there are any special conditions or caveats *before* you start work

What is a development plan?

You won't get too far on your journey into the planning system before you encounter the development plan for your area. The development plan forms the basis of the planning system. This is a long-term plan produced by the local council that sets out how the area should be developed in the future. Typically, councils will look 10 to 15 years ahead. The development plan will contain proposals to accommodate the future needs of the community in terms of housing, schools, jobs and transport, etc., and identify how the more sensitive areas should be safeguarded from development.

WHAT IS A DEVELOPMENT PLAN?

The plans are prepared by local councils in consultation with local residents and businesses and other stakeholders who have an interest in the future of their area.

Your Local Development Plan is an important reference point for you in providing an indication of the future shape of the area and also for commercial developers in establishing where and how developments can take place. The plan is also the key tool for councils in determining whether or not individual planning applications are acceptable. Decisions on planning applications must always be taken in accordance with the provisions of the development plan unless material considerations dictate otherwise.

The development plan system has recently been overhauled and now consists of a series of documents which comprise:

- a core strategy setting out the vision and objectives for the area;
- site specific allocations and policies;
- a proposals map;
- supplementary planning documents which provide further details on specific policies in the development plan documents or site allocations;
- a statement of community involvement setting out how local residents and the business community should be involved in the preparation of the development plan documents and in the processing of individual planning applications;
- a sustainability appraisal which assesses how sustainable the development plan documents are in meeting the current needs of the community but without compromising the needs of future generations;

FREQUENTLY ASKED QUESTIONS

- a local development scheme which details the council's programme for the preparation of the development plan documents;
- area action plans which contain detailed proposals for individual areas that are proposed for significant change; and
- an annual monitoring report which sets out how the development plan documents are achieving their targets and objectives.

Collectively, these documents are referred to as the Local Development Framework and will eventually replace the current Local and Unitary Development Plans that all councils have already adopted.

Generally, there are four stages in the preparation of most of these new development plan documents, although not every document is required to be subject to independent examination:

- survey and gathering of information;
- consultation;
- independent examination; and
- adoption.

As a homeowner, you will probably be more interested in the consultation stage relating to specific proposals for individual sites, e.g. housing, industry or shops, rather than in the formulation of strategy and more general objectives within the LDF process. Getting involved in consultations about site allocations will help to ensure that any specific land use allocations for new housing, industry, roads or shops, etc., that are proposed in your area do not adversely impact your home.

What is a dwelling?

In planning, the term 'dwelling' or 'dwellinghouse' covers houses and bungalows, whether semi-detached, detached

WHAT IS A DWELLING?

or terraced. A terraced house is defined as three or more dwellings joined by party walls (shared walls), or having adjoining walls.

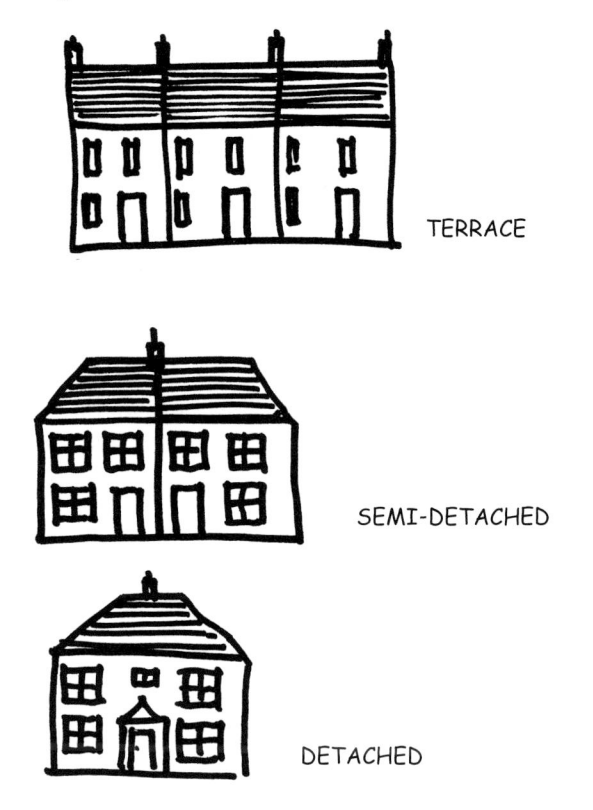

TERRACE

SEMI-DETACHED

DETACHED

Types of houses

Most importantly, there is an important distinction between dwellings and flats for the purposes of determining whether development is permitted or not. A dwelling does not include a building containing one or more flats, or a flat contained within such a building. Almost all of the Permitted Development rights apply to dwellings only. So, owners and occupiers of flats have limited Permitted Development rights which apply only in respect of the installation of satellite dishes, microgeneration equipment and advertisements.

For simplicity, any reference to 'house' or 'home' throughout this book covers all types and forms of dwelling.

What is the 'original building'?

The 'original building' is defined as the building that existed on 1 July 1948 or, if built after this date, the building as it was first built. This is an important concept because the 'original' building is the basis for assessing whether the extensions or alterations that you are proposing are Permitted Development.

Tying in any permitted allowances to the original building in this way ensures that a Permitted Development allowance can only be exercised once on the same house. It therefore applies to the house and not the owner or occupier. So, if a previous owner of your house carried out any building work, your Permitted Development entitlement may have been used up.

What is the curtilage of a dwelling?

The curtilage is the area of land around the house that you own or rent. Within the curtilage, you are allowed to use land or buildings in a manner that is incidental to the enjoyment of your home without the need for planning permission.

Unfortunately, there is no precise definition of curtilage. Often, the curtilage of a house will be self-evident and include your garden, yard or the piece of land on which your home is sited. It will frequently comprise the land identified on your deeds as forming your garden and the land belonging to you. However, the curtilage does not have to be enclosed or marked and can in some cases be detached from the house as long as it can be proved that the area of land serves your home in some reasonably useful manner.

It has been left to the courts to clarify how the curtilage of a house should be determined. In practice, three tests have been applied:

- physical layout;
- ownership past and present; and
- uses past and present.

So, land that is separated from a house can still form part of its curtilage providing that there is some association to link it to the house. Ultimately, every case will be judged on its merits. It is, however, an important concept to establish because the Permitted Development rights apply only to buildings or the use of land within the curtilage of your home.

The curtilage of your home will therefore usually correspond to your garden. Only in a very few cases will a garden be separate and, in this instance, you will have to consider the relationship between your home and the land and how it has been used in the past to demonstrate that it now forms part of your garden.

What are 'purposes incidental' to the enjoyment of a dwelling?

This is a key phrase to determine whether the use of land or a building within your garden is Permitted Development. There is no precise definition of 'purposes incidental', but the planning regulations confirm that such uses can include the keeping of poultry, bees, pet animals, birds or other livestock for the domestic needs or personal enjoyment of the occupants of the dwelling.

Generally, for a use to be considered incidental it must be subordinate to the enjoyment of your home. There are no hard and fast rules and each case will be different and depend on the nature and scale of the activity proposed. For example, if you use a shed in the garden for painting as a hobby, this forms part of the enjoyment of your home. However, if you were then to use the same shed to display and sell your paintings, this would be more akin to a business and would no longer be ancillary to the enjoyment of your home.

What are the Use Classes?

Most buildings are grouped into classes according to their use. For example, there are different classes of use for shops, restaurants, cafes, public houses and other types of businesses. In total, there are 14 classes covering a wide variety of different uses. Dwellings are classified as Use Class C3. This class covers use of a building as a dwelling-house whether by a single person or by people living together as a family; or by no more than six residents living together as a single household, including a household where care is provided for residents. The Use Class applies whether the dwelling is used as the sole or main residence or as a second home.

Changing the use within the same Use Class is allowed under the Permitted Development rights. For example, a hairdressers and a post office both fall within Use Class A1 and one could change to the other without the need for planning permission. Some changes of use are also permitted between the different Use Classes. So, a betting office, which is Use Class A2, could change to a shop (Use Class A1) without planning permission.

Not every type of use is assigned a Use Class, and those that aren't are known as *sui generis* uses, which literally means 'of its own kind'. Theatres, petrol filling stations and shops selling and/or displaying motor vehicles are examples of *sui generis* uses.

What is a highway?

Many of the Permitted Development rights affecting individual houses refer to proximity to and relationship with an adjoining highway. For these purposes, a highway includes a public road, footpath, bridleway and byway. Highway has a much wider meaning than simply a road used by vehicles, so bear this in mind when assessing whether your development is permitted or not. For example, if your home has a public footpath running down the side of it, this footpath will count as a highway for the purposes of working out your Permitted Development entitlements.

It is important to note that the highway in question must be a public highway. A private access road is not generally considered a highway for the purposes of determining Permitted Development rights.

What is a listed building?

Some buildings are statutory listed for their special architectural or historic interest. Buildings are graded according to their rarity or quality – grade I, grade II* and grade II, with grade I representing the highest and potentially the most nationally or internationally important buildings.

Buildings that are listed will be identified on the local land charges search undertaken prior to the purchase of a property. Alternatively, if there is any doubt whether a building is listed, check with your local council. Most councils hold a schedule of listed buildings in their area.

Consent is required for demolition of a listed building and for any works of alteration or extension that would affect its character as a building of special architectural or historic interest. This is a separate consent (known as Listed Building Consent) over and above the planning permission and applies to all works, both internal and external. Repairs to a listed building do not normally require consent unless they involve alterations that would affect its character. To assist in understanding what comprises the character of a listed building, each listing entry contains a description of features of special architectural or historic interest. However, the listing entry is not definitive in identifying important features and should not be relied upon to determine whether proposed works will require Listed Building Consent.

The extent of the listing also includes any object or structure that is fixed to the building or located within grounds of the building and which has been there since 1 July 1948. This is called a 'curtilage listing'.

So, if you own or occupy a listed building and are proposing to undertake any building works, you may find that, although planning permission is not required, you might still need to obtain Listed Building Consent. It is a criminal offence to undertake works to a listed building without the prior consent of the council and, unlike the planning regime, consent may also be required for any works to the interior of the building. Such works could involve the removal of internal panelling, a staircase or a cornice and, if these are identified as features of architectural or historic interest, Listed Building Consent will be required.

In some areas, councils hold local lists of buildings of architectural or historic interest, although these have no statutory force and are not subject to the Listed Building Consent procedures. They are, however, indicative of a local historic interest and so extra sensitivity is required in the preparation of any development proposals for these properties.

⚠ It is a criminal offence to carry out works on a listed building without the prior consent of the council. Listed Building Consent may also be needed for interior as well as exterior works

What is a conservation area?

Conservation areas are designated because of their special architectural or historic interest. All buildings

WHAT IS A CONSERVATION AREA?

located within a conservation area are subject to greater restrictions on Permitted Development rights. Also, for any home located within a conservation area, there is an additional requirement to obtain permission to undertake demolition of most structures and to undertake any works to trees located in the area. There are exceptions and you will not need to notify the council if the tree is less than 7.5 centimetres in diameter when measured at a point 1.5 metres above ground level, or 10 centimetres in diameter if the work only involves thinning to help the growth of other trees. In addition, you will not need to obtain the council's consent to demolish a building which has a cubic content of less than 115 cubic metres or to demolish any gate, wall or fence that is either less than 1 metre in height and adjoins a highway, or 2 metres in height if it does not.

In some conservation areas, the council may have imposed an Article 4 Direction, which further restricts the developments that can be undertaken without planning permission. Under the planning regulations, councils have powers to make an Article 4 Direction which removes the Permitted Development rights within a defined area because of the impact such development could have on the character of the area.

Responsibility for designating conservation areas rests with local councils, so your local council is the appropriate authority to confirm whether your home is located within a conservation area. Normally the existence of a conservation area or an Article 4 Direction will be identified in the local land charges search undertaken prior to the purchase of your home.

Any proposal to designate a new conservation area or to declare an Article 4 Direction will be subject to advance notification and, therefore, prior consultation will take place with property owners who may be affected by such an order. So your council will notify you if they are proposing to designate a conservation area or to increase controls over development within an existing conservation area.

What is a Scheduled Ancient Monument?

Some ancient monuments are identified on a national schedule of ancient monuments. Any works that are likely to result in the demolition, destruction, damage, removal, repair, alteration or addition to a monument or result in flooding, tipping in, on or under a scheduled monument will require Scheduled Ancient Monument Consent. This consent must be obtained in addition to any planning permission, Listed Building Consent or Conservation Area Consent that is also required.

Consent is obtained from the secretary of state for culture, media and sport in consultation with English Heritage. Applications for consent must contain full details of the proposed works. The websites of both the Department for Culture, Media and Sport (www.culture.gov.uk) and English Heritage (www.english-heritage.org.uk) contain useful guidance on the implications of a Scheduled Ancient Monument and the procedure for obtaining consent.

Your local council should keep a list of Scheduled Ancient Monuments in your area. Alternatively, some county councils are responsible for archaeological advisory services, so they may also keep records.

It is most unlikely that your home is located within or close to a Scheduled Ancient Monument. If it is, this will be obvious from the presence of some form of historic feature or ruin in, or close to, your garden.

Who is my local planning authority?

The planning process is administered by local planning authorities. Generally this is the council to whom you pay your council tax and invariably will be the local borough or district council. In London, the planning authority is the borough council. County councils do have planning powers, but these are restricted to strategic matters and planning for waste and minerals. County councils are also responsible in most areas for highway matters and so you may come across them in their capacity for advising the local council on highway issues.

In Wales and Scotland, the local planning authorities are the county and county borough councils. In Northern Ireland, the planning service is administered by the Department of the Environment, but individual district and borough councils are consulted on planning applications.

If your home is located within a National Park or within the Norfolk and Suffolk Broads, the local planning authority will be either the relevant National Park or Broads Authority. In some areas, urban development corporations have been set up with planning powers, but these are usually restricted to major development proposals rather than ones concerning individual dwellings.

The secretary of state for communities and local government has overall responsibility for administering the planning system. Intervention by the secretary of state in the day-to-day operation of the system, however, is limited to appeals, approval of some development plan documents and the issuing of national policy advice and guidance. Your involvement with the planning system will therefore be mostly directed at your local council

You will find a full list of all local planning authorities in England and Wales at the back of the book together with contact details and website addresses. Throughout this book the local planning authority is often referred to as 'the council' or 'your local council'.

⇨ List of local planning authorities in England and Wales **page 155**

FREQUENTLY ASKED QUESTIONS

What is Article 1(5) land?

Article 1(5) land is defined in the planning regulations as land in:

- a National Park;
- an Area of Outstanding Natural Beauty (AONB);
- a conservation area;
- an area specified under section 41(3) of the *Wildlife and Countryside Act* 1981;
- the Broads; and
- a World Heritage site.

If you live in any of these areas, your Permitted Development rights will be restricted because of the environmental sensitivity of the area. Your local council will normally be able to confirm whether your house is located within any of the above locations. The local land charges search undertaken at the time of purchase may also record the existence of such an area. Any new designation subsequent to the purchase or occupation of your home will be subject to consultation and notification, so you will receive advance notification of any change in the designation of the area in which your home is located or in the land surrounding it.

There are 15 National Parks in England, Wales and Scotland. These are:

- Brecon Beacons;
- Broads;
- Cairngorms;
- Dartmoor;
- Exmoor;
- Lake District;

- Loch Lomond;
- New Forest;
- Northumberland;
- North York Moors;
- Peak District;
- Pembrokeshire Coastal;
- Snowdonia;
- South Downs (see note below); and
- Yorkshire Dales.

The South Downs was designated as a National Park in March 2009. The new National Park Authority is to be set up in 2010 and will become fully operational by 2011.

The Broads is equivalent to a National Park. Information on the Broads can be obtained from www.broads-authority.gov.uk. Information on the National Parks can be obtained on www.nationalparks.gov.uk and this website includes maps that allow you to confirm whether your home is located within a National Park.

There are 878 World Heritage sites throughout the world, of which 27 are located within the UK. A list of these sites is available on whc.unesco.org.

⇨ More on conservation areas **page 22**

What is an advertisement?

The term advertisement is wide ranging and includes posters and notices; placards and boards; fascia signs and projecting signs; pole signs and canopy signs; models and devices; advance signs and directional signs; estate agents boards; captive balloon advertising; flags; price markers and price displays; traffic signs and town and village name signs.

FREQUENTLY ASKED QUESTIONS

If you wish to display an advertisement at your home, you may need to obtain Advertisement Consent from your council and this is separate from planning permission. Displaying the name of your house or displaying a sign indicating the presence of some business activity at your home, e.g. chiropody, tutoring or hairdressing, is considered an advertisement. Putting up a 'beware of the dog' notice or a for sale sign also counts as an advertisement.

In much the same way as some development is already permitted, so are some advertisements. They are then automatically outside the control of the council. Other advertisements are granted 'deemed consent' by virtue of the advertisement regulations and, again, do not require consent providing that certain conditions are met. Advertisements that are granted 'deemed consent' and which you might wish to display are described in detail in chapter 6.

When you display an advertisement the following five rules apply.

- You must keep them clean and tidy.
- You must keep them in a safe condition.
- You must not display them without the landowners consent.
- You must not display a sign that would obscure or hinder the interpretation of any official road, rail, waterway or aircraft signs or cause hazard to these types of transport.
- You must remove the sign if asked to do so by the council.

So, for example, if your advert were to come loose and pose a danger to passing pedestrians, you may be required to remove it or to make it safe. Similarly, if you put up a sign on the public highway without the permission of the highway authority, you will be asked to take it down.

⇨ Details of advertisements with deemed consent **page 67**

What is an Area of Special Control of Advertisements?

As with special areas where Permitted Development rights are more restrictive, limits are placed on Areas of Special Control of Advertisements, and you will not be allowed to display the full range of advertisements without obtaining prior consent from the council.

An Area of Special Control of Advertisements is designated by the council where the nature of the area has particular qualities that justify a stricter level of control over the display of advertisements. These areas are usually of scenic, historic, architectural or cultural value.

In an Area of Special Control, public notices and advertisements can still be displayed within a building, but the scope and extent of advertisements that are deemed to have consent may be restricted. Individual councils have the power to designate an Area of Special Control and to stipulate the variations to the categories of advertisement that would ordinarily be granted deemed consent. For example, in some urban areas, Areas of Special Control have been designated to limit the number of estate agents boards that can be displayed at any one property.

What is an Environmental Impact Assessment?

It is most unlikely that the development you are planning will require an Environmental Impact Assessment (EIA), but you may still come across the term as you navigate your way through the planning system.

FREQUENTLY ASKED QUESTIONS

An EIA is a process whereby the environmental impacts of a development project are identified, assessed and mitigated for. The process applies to major development projects. For some of these an EIA is mandatory, while for others it is discretionary and determined by the scale of the development and the environmental sensitivities of the location. A development project that involves the alteration of or extension to a single house or the construction of a building in the garden will not require an EIA, even if the house or building is located within an environmentally sensitive location such as the green belt.

In the rare event that your contact with the planning system throws up the question of an EIA, e.g. because your house is located within a Site of Special Scientific Interest or in or near a Scheduled Ancient Monument, you can apply to your council for a 'Screening Opinion'. This will provide you with a definitive view as to whether your building project requires an EIA or not. You will need to make your application in writing and enclose a plan identifying the land, a brief description of what you are proposing to do and any additional information or representations to explain the proposals and why you consider an EIA is not required. The council has three weeks to respond to your request, although it can ask for this period to be extended. If the council issues an opinion and you are not satisfied with it, or if the council fails to respond within the three weeks' statutory timescale, you have the right to appeal to the secretary of state.

The likelihood of your requiring an EIA for a development associated with your home is rare, but should the situation arise, the opportunity to apply for a Screening Opinion is a useful device to test the legality of the council's request. And, having a Screening Opinion from the council confirming that an EIA is not required is also very useful should anyone else object to your proposal on these grounds.

WHAT IS A TREE PRESERVATION ORDER?

⇨ What is a Site of Special Scientific Interest? **page 203**

⇨ What is a Scheduled Ancient Monument? **page 24**

What is a Tree Preservation Order?

Councils have powers to impose a Tree Preservation Order (TPO) on individual trees or groups of trees. A TPO can apply to a single tree or a group of trees, but not to hedges, bushes or shrubs. If a TPO is in place, it is an offence to cut down, top, lop, uproot, wilfully damage or destroy the protected tree without first obtaining permission from the council.

Tree Preservation Orders are usually made to protect trees that make a significant contribution to the local environment. If the council is considering making an order, it is required to serve notice on the owner of the tree or group of trees and any other interested person. So, if the council has identified that a TPO should be imposed on any tree or trees in your garden, you will receive prior notice of this and have the right to object to the making of the order. The council will take your comments into account before confirming the order. It is a criminal offence to carry out work to deliberately destroy or damage a tree that is protected by a TPO. Any offence committed will result in a prosecution in the magistrates' court and the maximum fine that can be imposed is £20,000.

Occasionally, the council may proceed with a TPO that has immediate effect and which will remain in force for six months, after which the council has to confirm that the order will become permanent. This procedure is often used when there is an immediate threat to trees that are of environmental importance. Consultation will take place with the owners and occupiers of the land of the trees in question and any comments received will be considered before the council makes the decision on whether to confirm the TPO.

FREQUENTLY ASKED QUESTIONS

⚠ Deliberately destroying or damaging a tree that is protected by a TPO is a criminal offence and will result in a prosecution

Who can apply for planning permission?

Surprisingly, anybody can apply for planning permission even if they do not own the property or the land concerned. For instance, if you are a potential purchaser of a property, you could apply even though you do not have the legal papers confirming ownership. If you are not the owner of the property but wish to make an application, your only obligation is to serve a notice of any planning application on the person or persons who owned the property 21 days before the date when you submit your application.

Freeholders, and leaseholders who have a lease of seven years or more, are considered the owners for the purposes of the planning Acts.

What happens if I live in Scotland, Wales or Northern Ireland?

The principle that any person who wishes to carry out some form of development must apply for planning permission also applies in Scotland, Wales and Northern Ireland. Likewise, some forms of development undertaken by homeowners are already permitted by government order or regulation, but the orders and regulations that are in place in England do not extend to Scotland and Northern Ireland and, in some more limited cases, Wales.

So, if you live in Scotland, Wales or Northern Ireland, although the concept of development and Permitted Development is the same as in England, the precise details of what is permitted, which authority to apply to and with whom to challenge any decision is different. Regulations are also specific to each country. Similarly, the development plan system that operates in Scotland, Wales and Northern Ireland is different from that operating in England, with greater emphasis on a national plan. Government policy, guidance and advice are also specific to each country.

Will I need assistance?

This is a critical question for you as you plan your building work. The degree of assistance that you require will, to some extent, depend on the complexity of your project and whether or not you will need planning permission or any other forms of approval or consent. You will certainly require the services of an architect or architectural technician to translate your ideas into drawings that can support a planning or Building Regulations application. Using the services of a planning consultant will ensure that your planning application is presented in a way that gives it the best possible chance of success. In addition, you may need to use a chartered surveyor if your proposal impacts on the Rights to Light enjoyed by your neighbour or if there is a potential breach of a Restrictive Covenant. A building surveyor will be useful if there are any party wall issues.

Once you have obtained all the requisite approvals for your project, you may want to use the services of a building contractor. You may also elect to retain the architect to oversee the building works. The local council will need to be satisfied that the work has been completed in accordance with planning and Building Regulations where such approvals are necessary. And your bank or building society may need proof that the work has been completed satisfactorily before they will release funds. It is important that your builder does not vary the plans that the council has approved. Should you change your mind about certain aspects of the project during the construction stages, make sure you notify the council. Otherwise, you

FREQUENTLY ASKED QUESTIONS

run the risk of action being taken against you by the council either under the planning or Building Regulations.

It is also important to retain copies of any approvals or consents obtained both before and during the building process. These documents will be invaluable if you decide to sell your home, as you will need to demonstrate to potential buyers and their solicitors that all the building work you have undertaken has been approved by the council and carried out in accordance with any planning requirements and, most importantly, Building Regulations. This information is now required for inclusion in the recently introduced Home Information Packs (HIPs). You will certainly want to avoid the situation where the information is requested but cannot be provided and a sale is jeopardised at a critical stage.

Finally, there are two more important allies to make your journey into the planning process easier. These are, firstly, the planning and building control departments of your local council that will be handling the respective approval processes; and, secondly, your neighbours, whom you will want on your side if you have to submit a planning application. Early contact with both the council officers and your neighbours is recommended and you should maintain regular contact with them throughout the approval and subsequent construction stages.

At the back of the book you will find a list of useful contacts to assist you in your building project.

⚠ Make sure your builder sticks to the approved plans or the council may take action against you or them under the planning or Building Regulations

➡ More about Rights to Light **page 85**

➡ More about Restrictive Covenants **page 81**

➡ More about party walls **page 78**

Will I need any other consents or approvals?

Even if you do not require planning permission, you may still need to obtain other consents or approvals, either from your council or, in some cases, from your neighbours.

The following checklist identifies other consents or approvals that might be required. Before you turn to the next chapter, work through this checklist to highlight anything that could be relevant to your home. The process for obtaining any additional consents or approvals is explained in greater detail in chapter 7.

⚠ Even if you have established that your proposed works don't require planning permission, check if you need any other consents or approvals

Checklist of other consents and approvals		
Questions for you	Where can I check?	What are the consequences?
Is your home listed?	Your local council will be able to confirm whether your house is statutorily listed.	If your home is listed, there are restrictions on the works you can undertake without planning permission. In addition, you will have to obtain Listed Building Consent to undertake any works of alteration and extension, even if planning permission is not required.

FREQUENTLY ASKED QUESTIONS

		The extent of listing can apply to buildings in your garden and, if you are planning any works to these buildings, you will also require Listed Building Consent.
Is your home located in a conservation area?	Your local council will be able to confirm whether your home is located within a conservation area. In addition, this will have been recorded on the land charges search when you purchased your home.	If your home is located within a conservation area, the Permitted Development rights are more restrictive. You will also need to obtain Conservation Area Consent for demolition and the felling, lopping or topping of trees in your garden.
Are there any restrictive conditions imposed on any previous planning permissions for your house?	This information will be apparent from the planning permission that was issued allowing the construction of the original house or any extensions or additions to the house. However, it does not apply to houses that pre-date the introduction of the planning system, i.e., houses that were constructed before 1 July 1948.	If there are restrictive conditions imposed on a planning permission, the individual wording and requirements of the conditions will determine the actions you need to take. It may be that you require the council's approval to undertake further building works that ordinarily would be Permitted Development.

WILL I NEED ANY OTHER CONSENTS OR APPROVALS?

	Your local council will hold records of all old planning decisions and these are accessible to the public. The format of the records varies from council to council; some will be held on microfilm, while others will be held on paper or in electronic format.	In this instance, you will have to submit an application to the council in the usual way to get permission to vary the terms of the condition.
Is my home subject to any Restrictive Covenants?	The existence of any Restrictive Covenants will be recorded on your deeds or on the Land Registry entry for your home. If you do not have a copy of your deeds, check if your solicitor, bank or building society holds them.	If your home is subject to a Restrictive Covenant that restricts the development you are able to carry out, then regardless of any Permitted Development provisions, you will have to apply for a relaxation of the covenant before proceeding with the work. Applications to modify a Restrictive Covenant are not made to your local council but to the Lands Tribunal. The Tribunal can be contacted at Procession House, 55 Ludgate Hill, London EC4M 7JW or at www.landstribunal.gov.uk

FREQUENTLY ASKED QUESTIONS

Is my home located in an area where an Article 4 Direction is in force?	Your local council will be able to confirm if your home is located within an area covered by an Article 4 Direction.	If you do live in a home where there is an Article 4 Direction in place, this will have the effect of removing what would otherwise be Permitted Development and you will have to apply to your local council for planning permission.
Is my home a dwelling?	There is an important distinction in planning terms between dwellings and flats. The answer should be self-evident, but the important distinction is whether the property is a single house, irrespective of whether it is a house or bungalow or detached, semi-detached or part of a terrace, or whether it forms part of a building containing one or more flats or apartments.	Generally, Permitted Development rights apply to dwellings only and so, if you home is located within a building containing one or more flats, you will need to obtain planning permission from the council for most works to the outside of the building.

WILL I NEED ANY OTHER CONSENTS OR APPROVALS?

Is my home located in a National Park, an Area of Outstanding Natural Beauty, a conservation area, the Broads, or a World Heritage site?	If it is, it will qualify as Article 1(5) land under the planning regulations. While most of these locations will be self-evident, if you are not sure, your local council will be able to confirm whether your house is located within any of these designations. The following website has information and maps on the location and extent of each National Park: www.nationalparks.gov.uk A list of World Heritage sites is available on: whc.unesco.org	The Permitted Development thresholds in these areas are generally lower than is standard, so you will need planning permission for some works.

FREQUENTLY ASKED QUESTIONS

Have any extensions or additions to my home been undertaken previously?	This should be self-evident. However, details of any alterations or extensions will be recorded on the land charges search that your solicitor carried out at the time of purchase. This will include any applications for planning and/or Building Regulations. You can also check the planning register held by your local council which will contain details of all previous planning applications submitted in respect of your home. Details of approvals under Building Regulations are also held by the local council, so check with this register, too.	If your home has been extended in the past, your Permitted Development entitlement may already have been used up. If this is the case, you will need to apply to the council for planning permission for any further works.

WILL I NEED ANY OTHER CONSENTS OR APPROVALS?

Is my home located in or near a Scheduled Ancient Monument?	Your local council will have a list of Scheduled Ancient Monuments in the area. Alternatively, a list of Scheduled Ancient Monuments may also be kept by the Archaeological Services Department of the county council.	If your home is in or near a Scheduled Ancient Monument, you will have to obtain consent from the secretary of state for any works that could damage, destroy, alter or flood the monument. This consent will be in addition to any planning permission, Listed Building Consent or Conservation Area Consent that is required.
Is my home located within an Area of Special Control of Advertisements?	Your local council will maintain a list of such areas. Alternatively, when you purchased your house, the existence of an Area of Special Control will have been highlighted.	If your house is located within an Area of Special Control of Advertisements, there will be stricter controls over the display of advertisements. For example, there may be a restriction on the number of estate agents boards that can be displayed when selling your home.
Are any trees in my garden subject to a TPO?	Your local council will have details of TPOs. In addition, the existence of a TPO will be recorded on the search of the local land charges register undertaken at the time of purchase.	If any trees within your garden are subject to a TPO, you will have to obtain consent from the council to undertake any works to the trees.

FREQUENTLY ASKED QUESTIONS

> ***Thinking! – some golden rules***
> - Seek professional and technical help where necessary
> - Consult your neighbours
> - Make contact with your local council planning department
> - Check what other consents you need
> - Check if your home is classified as a dwelling
> - Check if there are any other designations that affect your home

4 Measurements, dimensions and drawings

If your ideas for improving your home involve building work, these will have to be translated into a scaled drawing that shows how the new building relates to your home and to any neighbouring houses, and also what size it is. You will need this information not only for any approval process, but also to provide the blueprint for your builder.

What to measure – and how

It's important to be accurate because the overall size, height and location will determine whether or not you need planning permission. And, in the event that you obtain either planning or Building Regulations approval, you must ensure the work is carried out in accordance with the approved plans.

Measuring the floor area

For the purposes of determining whether your proposed work is allowed under the Permitted Development rights, the floor area measurements should be based on the gross external area (GEA). This is the floor area of the building measured externally, incorporating the thickness of the external walls and each floor level as well as any outbuildings providing these share at least one wall with the main building.

MEASUREMENTS, DIMENSIONS AND DRAWINGS

Measuring the height

The height of the building should be measured from the ground immediately adjacent to the building. Where the ground is uneven, the highest point of the adjacent land should be used.

Cubic measurements

Where a cubic measurement is required, i.e. the volume of any extension or enlargement, this should be based on the external envelope of the whole building, as above.

Converting to metric

All dimensions quoted in the planning regulations are metric. If you still use imperial measurements, the equivalent values of the commonly used dimensions are:

- 1 inch = 25.4 millimetres (mm) or 2.54 centimetres (cm)
- 1 foot = 0.3048 metres (m)
- 1 square foot = 0.0929 square metres (m^2)
- 1 cubic foot = 0.028 cubic metres (m^3)

You can convert from imperial to metric by using the following conversion rates:

- To convert inches to millimetres multiply by 25.4
- To convert feet to metres multiply by 0.3048
- To convert square feet to square metres multiply by 0.0929
- To convert cubic feet to cubic metres multiply by 0.028

Generally, you will find that the measurements required for determining Permitted Development thresholds are based on a linear measurement, i.e. a straight line from A to B, or

WHAT TO MEASURE – AND HOW

the area or the cubic content of both the existing and proposed new building. These are the three measurements that you will invariably need in order to establish whether your project requires planning permission.

> For a handy tool that lets you calculate the volume of a number of different kinds of buildings or extensions, go to:
> www.planningportal.gov.uk/uploads/volcalc/volcalc.html

The drawing requirements for both planning and Building Regulations applications are specific. Drawings must:

- be to scale;
- have elevations clearly marked as north, south, west and east;
- have a north point on layout and location plans;
- be clearly titled to identify the development project; and
- have a reference number so that the specific drawing can be identified and to enable any subsequent amendments to be referenced.

As a general guide, the appropriate scale to use for drawings is as follows:

- Location plans should be on a scale of 1:1250 or 1:2500.
- Site layout plans should be on a scale of 1:200 or 1:500.
- Existing and proposed floor plans and elevations should be on a scale of 1:50 or 1:100.

If you have no drawing expertise, you will need to get assistance. At the back of the book you will find useful contact details of services offering professional support.

MEASUREMENTS, DIMENSIONS AND DRAWINGS

⚠ Be accurate when measuring – the overall size, height and location will determine whether or not you need planning permission. Once you obtain planning or Building Regulations approval, you will not be able to deviate from the approved plans without the council's prior approval

5. What can I do without permission – in my home?

Enlarging, improving or altering your home

Scope of works

The enlargement, improvement or other alteration of your home. This includes extensions or additions such as adding a conservatory or an attached garage, or alterations and improvements such as creating a basement, inserting a bay window or replacing your windows, and converting your garage into a living room; but it *does not include* adding a verandah, balcony or raised platform; installing a microwave antenna, chimney, flue or soil and vent pipe; or altering any part of the roof.

You will not need planning permission, providing:

- the work results in less than 50 per cent of the ground area of your garden being covered by buildings;
- the height of any proposed new building is lower than the highest part of the existing house;
- the height of the eaves of the new building is lower than the eaves of the existing house (the eaves of your house is the overhang at the edge of your roof – see illustration on page 50);
- the new building does not extend beyond any wall of the existing house that fronts a highway and forms the principal or side elevation of the house;
- the new building will be single storey and extend beyond the rear wall of the house by less than 4 metres in the case of a detached house or by less than 3 metres for any other house, or will be less than 4 metres in height;

WHAT CAN I DO WITHOUT PERMISSION – IN MY HOME?

- the new building is more than one storey but does not extend beyond the rear wall of the existing house by more than 3 metres or is more than 7 metres from the boundary of the house;
- the new building is more than 2 metres from the boundary of the house and the height of the eaves is less than 3 metres; or
- the new building is less than 4 metres in height if it projects beyond a side elevation, is single storey and less than half the width of the original dwelling.

Further considerations

For properties located in a National Park, an Area of Outstanding Natural Beauty, a conservation area, the Norfolk Broads or a World Heritage site, works are not permitted if:

- they will consist of, or include, the cladding of any part of the exterior of the dwelling with stone, artificial stone, pebble dash, render, timber, plastic or tiles;
- the enlarged part of the house will extend beyond a wall forming the side elevation of the original dwelling; or
- the enlarged part of the dwelling will have more than one storey and extend beyond the rear wall of the original dwelling.

Any development that is permitted is subject to the following conditions.

- The materials you use in any exterior work (other than those used in the construction of a conservatory) must be of a similar appearance to those used in the construction of the exterior of the original house.
- Any upper floor window located in a wall or roof slope that forms a side elevation of the dwelling must be obscure-glazed and non-opening unless the parts of the window that can be opened will be more than 1.7 metres above the floor of the room in which the window is installed.
- Where the enlarged part of the dwelling has more than one storey, the roof pitch of the enlarged part must, as far as is practicable, be the same as the roof pitch of the original dwelling.
- Your house must be classified as a dwelling.

➪ What is a dwelling? **page 16**

ENLARGING, IMPROVING OR ALTERING YOUR HOME

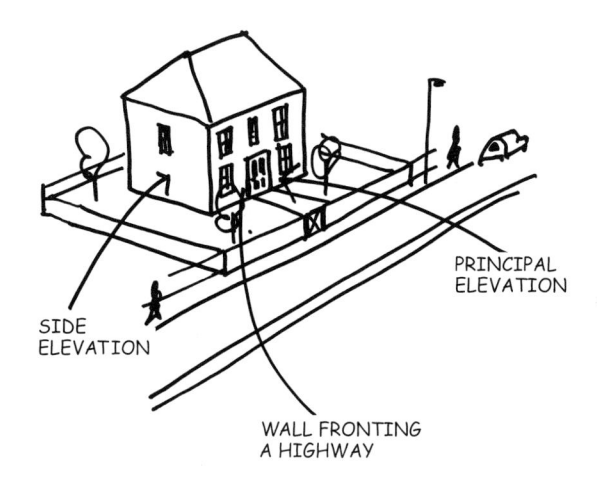

Overview of a typical house

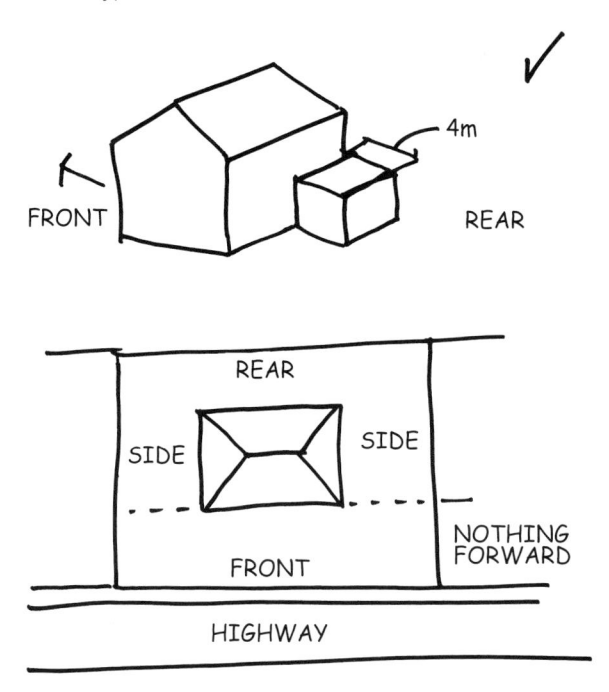

SIDE ELEVATION

PRINCIPAL ELEVATION

WALL FRONTING A HIGHWAY

4m

FRONT

REAR

✓

REAR

SIDE

SIDE

FRONT

NOTHING FORWARD

HIGHWAY

Enlarging or extending your home

49

WHAT CAN I DO WITHOUT PERMISSION – IN MY HOME?

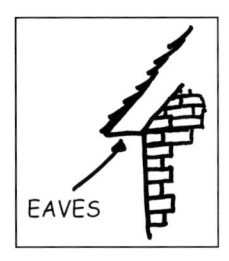

The eaves of a building

Adding a porch to your home

Scope of works

The construction of a porch outside any external door of your house.

You will not need planning permission, providing:

- the ground area of the porch is less than 3 square metres when measured externally;
- no part of the porch is more than 3 metres above ground level;
- no part of the porch is less than 2 metres from the boundary of a house that faces a highway; and
- your house is classified as a dwelling.

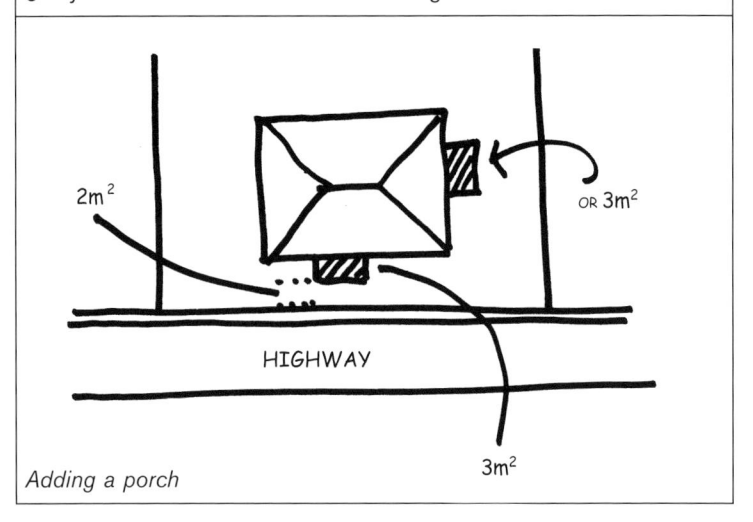

$2m^2$ OR $3m^2$

HIGHWAY

$3m^2$

Adding a porch

ALTERING THE ROOF OF YOUR HOME

Altering the roof of your home without changing its shape

Scope of works
Converting your loft without altering or extending the shape of the roof and installing roof lights or velux windows.

You will not need planning permission, providing:

- no part of the roof that you alter will protrude more than 150 millimetres above the slope of the existing roof when measured perpendicularly from the external surface of the original roof;
- the alteration does not exceed the highest part of the original roof;
- the alteration does not include the installation, alteration or replacement of a chimney, flue or soil and vent pipe;
- the alteration does not include the installation, alteration or replacement of solar photovoltaics or solar thermal equipment;
- any window located on a roof slope that forms the side elevation of your home is obscure-glazed and cannot be opened unless the parts of the window are more than 1.7 metres above the floor level of the room in which the window is to be installed; and
- your home is classified as a dwelling.

⇨ What is a dwelling? **page 16**

Enlarging your home by altering the shape of the roof

Scope of works
Extending or altering the roof, for example by adding a dormer window.

You will not need planning permission, providing:
• the alteration or addition will not be higher than the highest part of the existing roof; • the alteration or addition will not extend beyond the existing roof plane if this faces a highway and is the principal elevation of your house; • the cubic content of the resulting roof space is less than 40 cubic metres if your home is a terraced house, or 50 cubic metres for any other house; • it does not include a verandah, balcony or raised platform; • it does not include the installation, alteration or replacement of a chimney, flue or soil and vent pipe; • your home is classified as a dwelling; and • your home is not located within a National Park, an Area of Outstanding Natural Beauty, a conservation area, a World Heritage site or within the Broads.

Further considerations
• The materials you use in the exterior work must be of similar appearance to those on the existing house. • Wherever practicable, there should be at least 20 centimetres between the edge of the addition to your roof and the eaves of the original roof. • If you insert a window in the wall or the roof of the resulting addition and the window is on the side elevation, it should be obscure-glazed and non-opening unless the parts that can be opened are more than 1.7 metres from the floor level of the room in which the window is located.

ENLARGING YOUR HOME

Further considerations

- For the purposes of calculating the resulting roof space, this should include any enlargement of the original roof space whether permitted by this class or not. For example, the roof space may have been enlarged by building an extension to the house under the terms of Class A of the Permitted Development rights to enlarge, improve or alter your home and this has to be added for the purposes of calculating the overall increase in roof space.

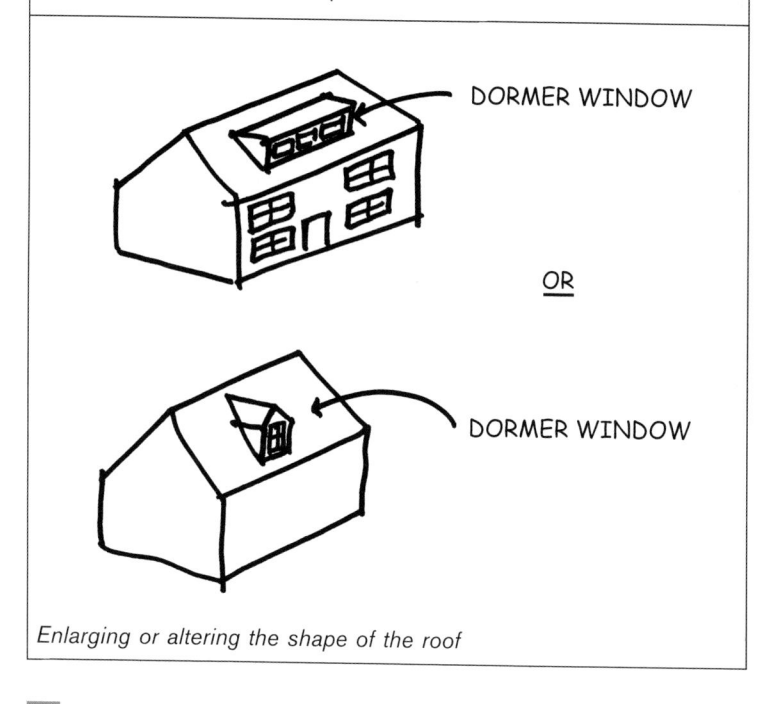

Enlarging or altering the shape of the roof

⇨ What is a dwelling? **page 16**

WHAT CAN I DO WITHOUT PERMISSION – IN MY HOME?

Adding solar panels & microgeneration equipment to your home or to a building in your garden

Scope of works

The installation, alteration or replacement of solar PV or solar equipment on your house or on a building within the curtilage of your dwellinghouse.
The installation, alteration or replacement of a flue that forms part of a biomass heating system on your house.
The installation, alteration or replacement of a flue that forms part of a combined heat and power system on your house.

You will not need planning permission, providing:

In the case of solar equipment
- the equipment does not project more than 200 millimetres beyond the wall or roof slope;
- the highest part of the solar equipment is lower than the highest part of the existing roof;
- the equipment is not located on the principal or side elevation or located on a building within the garden that is visible from the highway, if the property is located within a conservation area or World Heritage site.

In the case of the installation, alteration or replacement on a dwelling of a flue that forms part of a biomass heating or combined heat and power system
- the height of the flue is no more than 1 metre higher than the highest part of the roof of the existing dwelling;
- the flue is not on the principal or side elevation of the dwelling and visible from the highway, if the property is located within a conservation area or World Heritage site.

ADDING SOLAR PANELS & MICROGENERATION EQUIPMENT

Further considerations

- The Permitted Development limits for the installation of solar and microgeneration equipment apply to buildings containing flats as well as to dwellings.
- Solar PV means solar photovoltaics.
- Standalone solar means solar PV or solar thermal equipment that is not installed on a building.
- Microgeneration is defined in section 82(6) of the *Energy Act 2004* and means the use for the generation of electricity or the production of any heat which relies mainly on biomass, biofuels, fuel cells, photovoltaics, water (including waves and tides), wind, solar power, geothermal sources, combined heat and power systems and any other sources of energy that would cut the emission of greenhouse gases and where the capacity does not exceed 50 kilowatts for energy and 45 kilowatts thermal for heat.

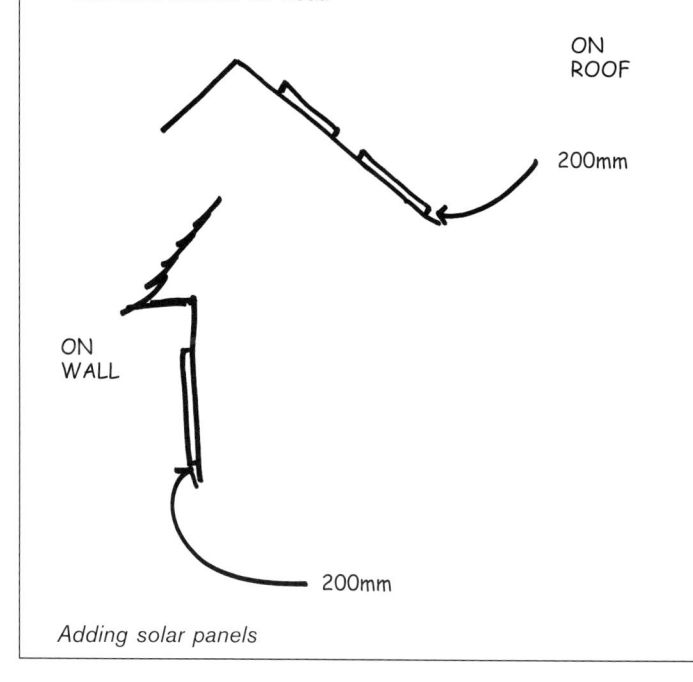

Adding solar panels

⇨ What is the curtilage of a dwelling? **page 18**

WHAT CAN I DO WITHOUT PERMISSION – IN MY HOME?

Working from home

Scope of works
Using any part of your home for your work or for business purposes. Examples include: renting out a bedroom; using a room for hairdressing or the provision of other medical services such as chiropody, reflexology, etc., teaching music or tutoring, dressmaking; or using any building in the garden for storing and/or repairing goods.

You will not need planning permission, providing:
• the overall character and use of the dwelling remains residential.

Further considerations
There is no hard and fast rule to determine whether working from home requires planning permission. In practice, it will depend upon the nature and extent of the work undertaken. For example, if you use one room in your house as an office or working area, then planning permission will not be required. The key tests that can be applied to determine whether the overall character of the house has changed from a residential use are as follows.<ul><li>Is the dwelling no longer your main residence?</li><li>Is there a significant increase in the number of people and vehicles that call at your house?</li><li>Are the activities involved in your business unusual for a residential area?</li><li>Are the activities associated with your business likely to cause nuisance in the form of noise or smells, particularly at unreasonable hours?</li></ul>Be aware that what starts out as a relatively low-key activity may grow with success and result in a significant increase in activity which then becomes the predominant use and requires planning permission. So, always ask yourself: is the dwelling still my home or has it become a business premise?

Subdividing or changing the use of your home

Scope of works
Subdividing your home into two or more separate dwelling units or changing the use to, for example, a restaurant or nursing home.

You will require planning permission:
• because the 1990 Act makes it clear that subdivision of an existing dwelling and a material change in the use of a building both comprise development for which planning permission is required. In the above examples, a change of use is involved and the existing and proposed uses are within different Use Classes.

Further considerations
• If your property is already subdivided, planning permission may also be required to convert it back to a single property. In some council areas this may be a sensitive proposal because it will result in the loss of smaller housing units. In this instance, the change is considered to be material because it conflicts with a local policy that protects smaller residential units. There is no hard and fast rule for determining whether a change from several dwelling units to one unit will require planning permission and much will depend on local policies. • Changes of use that involve some level of commercial activity may also be sensitive because of the impact on any neighbouring residential area.

⇨ What are the Use Classes? **page 20**

Painting your home

Scope of works

The painting of the exterior of any building or work by the application of any colour.

You will not need planning permission, providing:

- the painting is not for the purpose of advertisement, announcement or direction.

Further considerations

- The allowance for painting extends to buildings containing flats as well as to single houses.
- If your home is a listed building, then painting or re-painting may require Listed Building Consent if it is likely to affect the character of the building.

Installing chimneys, flues, soil and vent pipes on your house

Scope of works

The installation, alteration or replacement of a chimney, flue or soil and vent pipe on your house.

You will not need planning permission, providing:

- the height of the chimney, flue, soil and vent pipe does not exceed the highest part of the roof of your house by more than 1 metre;
- the chimney, flue or soil and vent pipe will not be located on a wall or roof slope that fronts a highway and forms the principal elevation or side elevation of your house if your home is located within a World Heritage site, a National Park, a conservation area, the Broads or within an Area of Outstanding Natural Beauty; and
- your house is classified as a dwelling.

⇨ What is a dwelling? **page 16**

Installing a microwave antenna on your house or within your garden

Scope of works

The installation, alteration or replacement of a microwave antenna on your house or within your garden. A microwave antenna includes a satellite dish used for radio, TV or data communications.

You will not need planning permission, providing:

- there will be no more than two antennas on the house or in the garden;
- an antenna will be less than 100 centimetres in length, in the case of a single antenna;
- it would not result in two antennas that do not meet the relevant size requirements;
- any antenna installed on a chimney is less than 60 centimetres in length;
- any antenna installed on a chimney does not protrude above the chimney;
- the antenna has a cubic capacity of less than 35 litres;
- the antenna is to be installed on a roof without a chimney and its highest part will be lower than the highest part of the roof;
- the antenna is to be installed on a roof with a chimney and the highest part of the antenna will be lower than the highest part of the chimney or a height 60 centimetres above the ridge of the roof, whichever is the higher;
- the antenna will not be located on a roof, chimney or wall that is visible from a highway or on a building that exceeds 15 metres in height if your home is located within a World Heritage site, a National Park, a conservation area, the Broads or within an Area of Outstanding Natural Beauty;
- the antenna will not be located on a roof, chimney or wall that is visible from a waterway or on a building that exceeds 15 metres in height if your home is located within the Broads; and
- your home is classified as a dwelling.

WHAT CAN I DO WITHOUT PERMISSION – IN MY HOME?

Further considerations
• Antennas are permitted in the above circumstances, providing that, as far as is practicable, they are located so as to minimise the effect on the external appearance of the building.
• Any antenna that is no longer needed for reception or transmission purposes must be removed as soon as is reasonably practicable.
• In terms of size, where two antennas are installed only one can exceed 60 centimetres in length; and in this instance any antenna which exceeds 60 centimetres must not exceed 100 centimetres in length.
• For the purposes of measuring the length of the antenna, a linear dimension is used and this is exclusive of any projecting feed element, reinforcing rim, mounting or bracket.

⇨ What is a dwelling? **page 16**

Demolishing any building or structure at your home

Scope of works
The demolition or partial demolition of any building or structure at your home or within the garden. This includes your house and, for example, any sheds, conservatories, walls, fences, storage tanks, swimming pools or carports.
You will not need planning permission, providing:
• the building is not a listed building, Scheduled Ancient Monument or is not located within a conservation area;

DEMOLISHING ANY BUILDING OR STRUCTURE AT YOUR HOME

- the building is a not dwelling* or does not adjoin a dwelling and has not been made unsafe or uninhabitable by deliberate action or neglect or if it could not be made secure through temporary repairs or support.

Further considerations

- Even if planning permission is not necessary, you may need to notify your local council of the proposed works of demolition under the provisions of the *Building Act* 1984 (as amended).
- Listed Building Consent is required for any demolition works that will impact on a listed building or its setting.
- Conservation Area Consent will be required for the demolition of all buildings or structures located within a conservation area and where the external volume exceeds 50 cubic metres.
- *A dwelling for the purposes of demolition works includes residential homes or hostels and buildings containing one or more flats.

6 What can I do without permission – in my garden?

Erecting gates, walls and fences

Scope of works
The erection, construction, maintenance, improvement or alteration of a gate, wall, fence or other means of enclosure around your home.
You will not need planning permission, providing:
• any gate, wall, fence or other means of enclosure that is adjacent to a highway used by vehicular traffic is less than 1 metre in height; • any gate, wall, fence or other means of enclosure that is not adjacent to a highway used by vehicular traffic is less than 2 metres in height; • any gate, wall, fence or other means of enclosure maintained, improved or altered is less than its former height or less than 1 metre if it is adjacent to a highway or does not exceed 2 metres in any other case; and • it is not within the curtilage of, or does not surround, a listed building.
Further considerations
• These Permitted Development rights apply generally to all buildings and not just to dwellings.

PLANTING HEDGES AND TREES IN YOUR GARDEN

- In determining what is adjacent to a highway, the ordinary meaning of 'adjacent' should be applied. So, for example, if the boundary is at right angles to the highway and adjoins the highway, the restrictions on height will apply to the first section of the fence or wall that adjoins the highway.
- Remember that a highway includes a public footpath, bridleway and byway, so if a public footpath runs down the side of your home, you will only be able to construct a fence or wall of less than 1 metre in height along this boundary without planning permission.

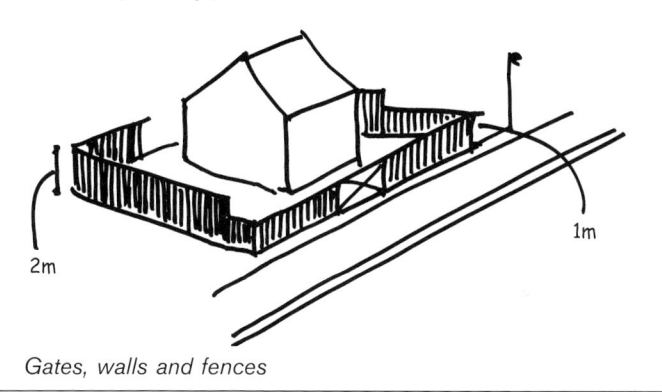

Gates, walls and fences

⇨ What is the curtilage of a dwelling? **page 18**

Planting hedges and trees in your garden

Scope of works
The planting of trees or hedges in your garden.
You will not need planning permission, providing:

- there is no condition on any planning permission for your home that restricts planting in specified areas of your garden. For example, where planning permission has been granted for a new vehicular access, a condition may have been imposed that restricts the height of any planting within the defined visibility splay from the access, in order that a driver pulling out of a driveway is able to see any approaching traffic or pedestrians.

WHAT CAN I DO WITHOUT PERMISSION – IN MY GARDEN?

Further considerations

- If your hedge encroaches on your neighbour's property (or vice versa), your neighbour is entitled to trim back the hedge to the boundary and return the trimmings to you. If the height of the hedge becomes excessive and restricts your access to daylight or sunlight, you should approach your neighbour in the first instance and try to persuade them to reduce the height. You are not entitled to reduce the height of the hedge without your neighbour's consent.
- If your neighbour does not respond to your request to reduce the height of the hedge, you can complain to your local council. In dealing with the complaint, the council will consider to what extent you have tried to resolve the matter amicably.
- If the height of the hedge is considered excessive, the council has the power to issue an order under the anti-social behaviour legislation requiring that the hedge be reduced to 2 metres in height. Failure to comply with the terms of the notice will result in a fine, although anyone served with such a notice has the right of appeal to the Planning Inspectorate.

Constructing a garden shed, summerhouse, greenhouse, swimming pool or other enclosure in your garden

Scope of works

The construction of any building or enclosure, swimming or other pool that will be used for purposes incidental to the enjoyment of your home. This includes a detached garage and a carport.

You will not need planning permission, providing:

- the total ground area covered by any buildings or enclosures does not exceed 50 per cent of your garden (excluding the ground area of the original house);

CONSTRUCTING A GARDEN SHED ETC. IN YOUR GARDEN

- no part of the new building or enclosure will be in front of the wall that forms part of principal elevation of the original house;
- the new building will have only one storey;
- the height of the building or enclosure is less than 4 metres in the case of a dual-pitched roof;
- the height of the new building is less than 2.5 metres if it is to be located within 2 metres from your boundary or less than 3 metres in any other case;
- the height of the eaves (see illustration overleaf) of the new building is less than 2.5 metres;
- the new building, enclosure or pool will not be located within the curtilage of a listed building;
- the new building, enclosure or pool will not include the provision of a verandah, balcony or raised platform;
- the new building would not result in the creation of a new dwelling or be used for the siting of a microwave antenna; and
- your home is classified as a dwelling.

Further considerations

- If your home is located within a World Heritage site, a National Park, an Area of Outstanding Natural Beauty or within the Broads, the total area of your garden that can be covered by buildings, tanks, enclosures and pools that are located more than 20 metres from the wall of your house should not exceed 10 square metres.
- If your home is located within a World Heritage site, a National Park, an Area of Outstanding Natural Beauty, a conservation area or within the Broads, no part of the building, enclosure or pool should be located between a wall that forms a side elevation of your house and the boundary of your garden.
- When calculating the total ground area coverage of any buildings, enclosures or pools, you should include any container that is used for the storage of oil or petroleum gas for domestic heating in your measurements.

Some definitions that may help

- The principal elevation means what you would normally consider to be the front of the house.
- A dual-pitched roof is one that contains a ridge and two slopes (see illustration overleaf).

WHAT CAN I DO WITHOUT PERMISSION – IN MY GARDEN?

> **Further assistance**
> - Details of which roads are classified or trunk roads can be obtained from the local highway authority.
>
> TWO SLOPES + DUAL-PITCHED ROOF RIDGE EAVES
>
> *Dual-pitched roof and eaves*

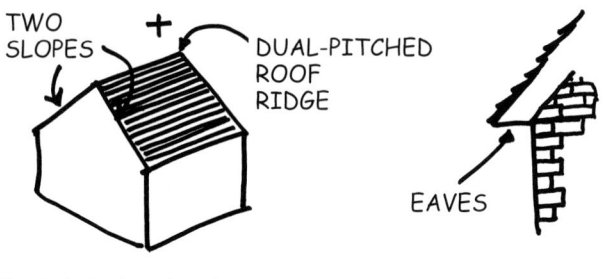

⇨ What are 'purposes incidental' to the enjoyment of your home?
page 19

Creating a new vehicular access to your home

Scope of works
The creation of a new vehicular access from an adjoining road.
You will not need planning permission, providing:
<ul><li>the access is to be created to a highway that is not a classified or trunk road; and</li><li>it is required in connection with a development that is already permitted.</li></ul>
You will need planning permission if:
<ul><li>you are creating a vehicular access to a classified road. In addition, you will need to obtain the consent of your local highway authority if it is necessary to cross over an existing footpath and reduce the height of a kerb to facilitate access by a car.</li></ul>

PLACING AN ADVERTISEMENT

Providing off street parking, driveways and hardstandings in the curtilage of your home

Scope of works
Paving front gardens to provide a hardstanding (a paved or other prepared surface) for parking a vehicle or to provide a more manageable surface; laying a patio and creating a driveway. This includes replacing existing hardstandings.
You will not need planning permission, providing that:
<ul><li>where the hard surface will be between the principal elevation of your house and a highway, the surface will be permeable, such as permeable concrete block paving or porous asphalt or gravel, or if the water is otherwise able to soak into the ground;</li><li>the area of the hard surface is less than 5 square metres; and</li><li>your home is classified as a dwelling.</li></ul>

⇨   What is the curtilage of a dwelling? **page 18**

Placing an advertisement on your home or in your garden

Scope of works
The display of an advertisement on your property or a directional sign to your property. Advertisements include advance or directional signs, estate agents boards and flags.
You will not require Advertisement Consent to display:
<ul><li>a name that is an integral part of the fabric of the building, e.g. the name of your property contained within the stonework above the front door;</li><li>a notice relating to a parliamentary election, although it must be removed 14 days after the election has taken place;</li></ul>

67

WHAT CAN I DO WITHOUT PERMISSION – IN MY GARDEN?

- the national flag of any country; the flag of the European Union, the Commonwealth or the United Nations; English county flags and saints flags associated with a particular county, as long as any flag does not carry any advertising (the erection of the flagpole in order to fly the flag may, however, require planning permission and also, in the case of listed buildings, Listed Building Consent).

Advertisement consent will not be required to display an advertisement on premises or buildings to which the notice or sign relates and that comprises any of the following.

- **A notice or sign displayed on the building or land to provide identification, direction or warning**. This includes the street number, name of the house and warning signs such as 'beware of the dog', 'please shut the gate' and 'no parking please'. The sign must not exceed 0.3 square metres in area or be illuminated and no letter or symbol on the advertisement should exceed 0.75 metres in height, or 0.3 metres if the property is located within an Area of Special Control of Advertisements.

- **A notice or sign indicating that a person, partnership or company is carrying on a profession, business or trade at the premises**, under certain circumstances. If you work from home, you are permitted to display a notice advertising this, subject to certain restrictions. For example, if you use one of the rooms in your house for hairdressing, you can display a notice advertising this, but the sign must not exceed 0.3 square metres in area. However, the display of a sign advertising that you are running a business from your house may confirm that the level of business use at your home exceeds what would normally be acceptable and, therefore, indicate that the business use requires planning permission. The notice or sign can only be illuminated if there are medical or similar services or supplies available at the premises. No letter or symbol on the advertisement should exceed 0.75 metres in height, or 0.3 metres if the property is located within an Area of Special Control of Advertisements.

PLACING AN ADVERTISEMENT

- **A notice or sign relating to a block of flats**, providing it does not exceed 1.2 square metres in area, although if there are two entrances on different road frontages a sign can be displayed at each entrance. The notice or sign can only be illuminated if there are medical or similar services or supplies available at the premises. No letter or symbol on the advertisement should exceed 0.75 metres in height, or 0.3 metres if the property is located within an Area of Special Control of Advertisements. No part of the advertisement should be more than 4.6 metres above ground level or more than 3.6 metres in an Area of Special Control of Advertisements.

Advertisement Consent will not be required to display temporary advertisements comprising the following.

- **Estate agents boards** advertising that a property is for sale or rent, providing that the board does not exceed 0.5 square metres in area or, in the case of two boards joined together, 0.6 square metres. The board must not project more than 1 metre from the wall of the building and only one board can be displayed on the property. The board must be removed within 14 days after the completion of the sale or the rental agreement.

- **A notice confirming that a firm or individual is carrying out building, engineering or construction works** at your property. This could include, for example, the name of the builder who is building your extension or the company installing double glazing. Only one firm may display a board and this should not exceed 2 square metres in area. One board of a larger size is permitted where there is more than one firm involved in the building works. The board can only be displayed while the works are taking place.

- **A sign advertising the sale of house contents**, providing that the board or notice does not exceed 1.2 square metres in area and is not displayed more than 28 days prior to the sale being held and 14 days after.

- **A temporary sign or notice advertising a local event being held for charitable and non-commercial purposes**. The event could be for religious, educational, cultural, political, social or recreational purposes and, for instance, include a church bazaar, school fete or sponsored marathon. The advertisement should not exceed 0.6 square metres in area and should not be displayed more than 28 days prior to the event taking place or 14 days after.

WHAT CAN I DO WITHOUT PERMISSION – IN MY GARDEN?

In the case of the above temporary advertisements, no letter, figure or symbol should:

- exceed 0.75 metres in height, or 0.3 metres in an Area of Special Control of Advertisements;
- be illuminated; or
- have the highest part of the advert at more than 4.6 metres above ground level, or more than 3.6 metres in an Area of Special Control of Advertisements, except for estate agents boards that relate to a building which is higher than this.

Properly authorised signs advertising approved Neighbourhood Watch and similar schemes can be displayed on or near highway land without Advertisement Consent, providing:

- they do not exceed 0.2 square metres in area;
- they do not exceed 3.6 metres above ground level;
- the permission of the local highway authority has been obtained if the sign is on highway land;
- notification is given to the council confirming the location of the sign 14 days prior to its erection and that the sign is properly authorised by the police and highway authority (if on their land); and
- the sign is removed within 14 days if the police or highway authority withdraws their approval or the Neighbourhood Watch scheme ceases to exist.

Further considerations

- There is a clear difference between the type of advertisements that are permitted within an Area of Special Control of Advertisements and those that are not. So it is important to check from the outset whether your property is located within such an area before assuming that you can proceed to erect a sign.

⇨ What is an advertisement? **page 27**

⇨ What is an Area of Special Control of Advertisements? **page 29**

Installing a standalone solar panel in your garden

Scope of works

The installation, alteration or replacement of a standalone solar panel or a water source heat pump within your garden.

You will not need planning permission, providing:

In the case of freestanding solar equipment which is installed, altered or replaced within your garden

- there is only one installation;
- the equipment is less than 4 metres in height when measured from ground level;
- it is not visible from the highway in the case of properties located within a conservation area or World Heritage site;
- it is more than 5 metres from your boundary;
- the curtilage is not that of a listed building; and
- the surface area of the panels is less than 9 square metres, or any dimension of its array (including any housing) is less than 3 square metres.

In the case of ground and water source systems, any system can be installed in your garden without the need for planning permission.

Further considerations

- The Permitted Development limits for the installation of solar and microgeneration equipment apply to flats and buildings containing flats as well as to dwellings.

⇨   What is the curtilage of a dwelling? **page 18**

Erecting a fuel tank or container in your garden

Scope of works

The erection of a container that is to be used for domestic heating purposes for the storage of oil or liquid petroleum gas within the curtilage of a dwellinghouse.

WHAT CAN I DO WITHOUT PERMISSION – IN MY GARDEN?

You will not need planning permission, providing:

- the total area of any container does not exceed 50 per cent of the total area of the curtilage of the dwelling;
- no part of the container is located in front of the wall that forms the principal elevation of the original dwellinghouse;
- the height of the container is less than 3 metres;
- the height of the container is less than 2.5 metres if it is located within 2 metres of the boundary of the curtilage of the dwelling;
- the container is not located within the curtilage of a listed building;
- the capacity of the container is less than 3,500 litres; and
- your home is classified as a dwelling.

Further considerations

- When measuring the total area of the curtilage of the dwelling, you should exclude the ground area of the original dwelling.
- If your home is located within a Word Heritage site, National Park, an Area of Outstanding Natural Beauty or the Broads, the total ground area of a container situated more than 20 metres from the house must not exceed 10 square metres.
- If your home is located within a Word Heritage site, National Park, an Area of Outstanding Natural Beauty, conservation area or the Broads, and the container will be situated between a side wall and the boundary of your garden, then permission will be required.

⇨ What is the curtilage of a dwelling? **page 18**

⇨ What is the principal elevation? **page 19**

⇨ What is the original building? **page 18**

7 I don't need planning permission – great! What do I do next?

Get confirmation from your council

If you are in any doubt as to whether the proposed extension or alteration to your home requires planning permission, you can seek to obtain a written opinion from the council. You can either request a letter from the council confirming the permitted status of your proposal or, alternatively, you can formally apply for a Certificate of Proposed Lawful Development or Use. The Certificate of Proposed Lawful Development or Use is a legal document and, therefore, a definitive and legal confirmation that the building work or use that you are proposing is Permitted Development and does not require planning permission. A letter issued by the council, on the other hand, will not carry the same legal status. An increasing number of councils, when faced with a request to confirm Permitted Development rights, are now asking for formal applications to be submitted.

Applying for a Certificate of Proposed Lawful Development or Use

You must apply in writing for the certificate and your application must contain sufficient factual information to allow the council to make a decision. You can apply by post or online using the government's planning website

I DON'T NEED PLANNING PERMISSION

(www.planningportal.gov.uk) or via the council's website (see list of council addresses at the back of the book).

If applying online, you should identify the application as 'an application for a Certificate of Proposed Lawful Development or Use' and then follow the step-by-step guide to give the information requested when prompted by the online form. In your application you will need to supply the following information:

- floor plans and elevations of what you are proposing that confirm the dimensions and relationship with your existing home and the property boundaries;

- confirmation of the details of the existing house, including floor areas, use and any previous extensions or alterations, and the year when the house was built;

- the location of your house – either the full postal address or a grid reference; and

- any other information that you consider is relevant and will help the council to reach a decision.

All the information can be submitted electronically; or you can submit the application form online and send the supporting documentation to the council by post. You can apply on your own or with professional or technical assistance. If you nominate an agent, the council will direct any correspondence to your agent rather than to yourself. If applying by post, the application form should be signed either by you, or by your agent on your behalf, and fully completed, including the certificate (on the application form) to confirm that you are the owner of the house or, if you are not the owner, that you have served notice of the application on the owner. If you apply online, it will be sufficient to type in your name to sign off when completing the application form.

As you are applying for confirmation that the work you are proposing at your home does not require planning

APPLYING FOR A CERTIFICATE

permission, the onus is on you or your advisers to supply all the necessary information to convince the council that a certificate should be issued.

The council will assess your application solely on the basis of what is proposed and the information submitted. In the case of Permitted Development, the planning merits of the proposed development are not relevant and only factual evidence about the history of the property and the dimensions and description of the proposed works will be considered.

You will have to pay a fee when the application is submitted. You can pay online, using a credit or debit card, or simply post a cheque to the council. The fee is based on half the standard fee for the equivalent planning application. In the case of enlargement, improvement or any other alteration of a house, this would be £75 based on the current fee regulations that came into force in April 2008. Planning application fees are subject to regular review and increases, so check with your council to find out the current rate for this category of application, or use the planning application fee calculator on the government's planning website (www.planningportal.gov.uk).

The council will base its decision on your application simply on whether the proposed works are Permitted Development or not. This limited process does not allow the council to make a judgment as to whether a development proposal accords with planning policy and that if a planning application were submitted, whether it would be granted. The council will either grant the certificate or refuse it wholly or in part and will not normally ask for further information or clarification about your application.

If your application is refused or the council fails to give you a decision within the statutory time period (eight weeks for householder applications), you have a right of

I DON'T NEED PLANNING PERMISSION

appeal. The rights of appeal and the appeal process are exactly the same as those outlined for planning appeals in chapter 9.

Obtaining a certificate that confirms your proposed development can be undertaken without planning permission is an important step. It will mean that you have a written certificate confirming the position and this will be an invaluable document if you decide to sell your home.

However, if you were to subsequently vary or change the nature of the works proposed, then the terms of the certificate may no longer apply and the works will not be covered. So, for instance, if you obtained a certificate confirming that working from home was based on a certain level of activity and this activity were to increase at a later date, this could take the use beyond the scope of the certificate.

⚠ Changing or varying the nature of your proposed works or use could render the terms of a Certificate of Proposed Development or Use invalid and the works or use would no longer be covered

➪ More on planning appeals **chapter 9**

Is your application complete?

Use the checklist below to make sure your application is complete and stands the best chance of getting the right result. Your application will not be validated if anything is missing.

Checklist for application for Certificate of Proposed Lawful Development or Use	
Complete the application form, sign and date it.	✔
Certify that you are the owner or that you have served notice on the owner.	✔

CHECK IF THERE IS ANYTHING ELSE TO CONSIDER

Provide a location plan of your house on a scale of 1:1250 or 1:2500; on the plan, identify your house in relation to two named roads and outline your property with a red line.	✓
Provide a site layout or block plan of what is proposed on a scale of 1:200 or 1:500.	✓
Provide elevations and sections of what is proposed on a scale of 1:50 or 1:100.	✓
Provide floor plans of both the existing building and the work that you propose on a scale of 1:50 or 1:100.	✓
Provide any further information to support your application. Remember that the onus is on you to persuade the council to issue a certificate confirming that what you propose is Permitted Development.	✓
Attach the application fee. At present £75 payable to the council.	✓

Check if there is anything else to consider before you proceed

You may have cleared the planning hurdle, but unfortunately there may be other consents or approvals that are required before you can proceed with the work. These are described below.

⚠ Even if you don't require planning permission, check if you need any other consents or approvals *before* you start your works

Building Regulations

Even though the planned works to extend or alter your home may be permitted under the planning Acts, you may still need to obtain approval under the Building Regulations. This is *separate to* planning permission, although it will be administered by the same council. The range of building work that is subject to the Building Regulations is far more extensive than that requiring planning permission, so even if you don't need planning permission, you may still have to obtain Building Regulations approval.

77

Building works that are subject to the Building Regulations include:

- the erection, extension or alteration of a building, including converting your loft space into living space;

- providing services and/or fittings in a building such as WCs, showers, washbasins, sinks, hot water cylinders, foul water and rainwater drainage, replacement windows and fuel burning appliance; and

- some changes of use, e.g. converting your garage into living space.

The Building Regulations are generally concerned with ensuring the health and safety of people in and around all types of buildings – domestic, commercial and industrial – energy conservation, and maintaining access to and use of buildings.

Responsibility for ensuring that any works comply with the Building Regulations rests with the person carrying out the works. So, if you are using a builder or contractor to carry out the works, the responsibility will be theirs. However, it is advisable to clarify that your builder or contractor will be addressing these issues before they start work, since any enforcement action taken for failure to comply with the regulations could also be targeted at you as the owner of the building. You (or your builder) must notify the council's building control section before you commence works and then as you reach key stages in the building process.

Party walls

A party wall is a shared wall, so if you live in a semi-detached or terraced house or bungalow or flat, you will share a wall, or walls, with your neighbour(s). If your proposed building work will directly affect a party wall or structure, you are required to give advance notice to the adjoining owners under the terms of the *Party Wall etc*

CHECK IF THERE IS ANYTHING ELSE TO CONSIDER

Act 1996. This requirement also applies to any building that straddles the boundary line between properties or work that involves excavation within 3 or 6 metres of a neighbouring building or structure, depending on the depth of the excavation.

You must give notice of your intention to carry out any building works that affect a party wall or structure at least two months prior to the works commencing and serve the notice on all adjoining owners. Persons who receive a Party Wall Notice can respond in writing that they are in agreement with the works proceeding or that they disagree with the works; or they can do nothing. If after 14 days of the notice being served, no response has been received, the parties will be deemed to be in dispute and the matter must be resolved by surveyors acting for the respective parties.

Parties who respond in writing can set out what additional or modified works are necessary to make the proposed works acceptable.

Party wall procedures are separate to both planning and Building Regulations approvals. So, even if you have already obtained both these approvals, you are still required to follow the party wall notification procedure before the approved work begins.

Although there is no enforcement mechanism for a failure to serve a Party Wall Notice, your neighbour can seek legal redress through a court injunction that can force the works to stop.

Bear in mind that you may also receive a Party Wall Notice from your neighbour and have to formally convey your agreement or disagreement to any building works that they are proposing.

⚠ If you fail to serve a Party Wall Notice, your neighbour can seek to stop the works through a court injunction

I DON'T NEED PLANNING PERMISSION

Planning conditions

In some cases, the original planning permission granting consent for the construction of your home may contain conditions that limit your right to add an extension to the house or restrict what you can build within your garden. Such conditions are usually imposed where the size of the plot is restricted or where uniformity of design is considered necessary, for example on a housing estate.

A typical condition will state:

> 'Notwithstanding the provisions of the Town and Country Planning (General Permitted Development) Order 1995 (or any order revoking and re-enacting that Order with or without modification), no development which would fall within Classes A to E in Part 1 of Schedule 2 to that Order shall be carried out without the prior written permission of the local planning authority.'

Conditions like this may legitimately be imposed on the planning permission issued for the main house and effectively remove the Permitted Development rights that the property owner would ordinarily enjoy. If this applies to your home, you will have to apply to the council to undertake building works that usually would be Permitted Development.

You may also find that other conditions have been imposed on an earlier planning permission that limit your right to undertake minor changes or that restrict your use of the house.

For example, a planning condition may require that a bathroom window is fitted with obscure glazing and be permanently fixed above a specified height to safeguard the amenity of an adjoining house. Conditions can also be imposed that restrict the use of a garage or parking space to the parking of private motor vehicles or that limit the use of any shed or outbuilding to storage for domestic use only. The reason for such conditions might be to prevent a garage or parking space being used for commercial purposes in the future or to limit the use of a building in a garden to one that is ancillary to the main house, e.g. a granny annex.

So, it is important to check that any previous planning permissions for your house do not include conditions that restrict your Permitted Development rights. The local land search carried out when you purchased your home will give details of the planning history for the property. Councils also maintain a register of past planning applications and these will identify any permissions and conditions that apply to your home. Increasingly, these are available in electronic format, so you may be able to access them via the council's website, although some councils still hold records only in paper format or microfilm. These planning records are available to the public, so do check with your local council to confirm how they are held and whether advance notice is required to make arrangements to inspect the planning records for your home.

If you find that the Permitted Development rights at your home have been limited or prohibited by a condition imposed on a previous planning permission, you will need to seek approval from the council to undertake the building work or to vary the terms of the condition. So you will have to prepare and submit a planning application to the council to seek approval for any proposed works that, in normal circumstances, would be allowed under Permitted Development.

⇨ How to prepare and submit a planning application **chapter 8**

Restrictive Covenants

Your home may be subject to a Restrictive Covenant. Restrictive Covenants are private agreements between landowners that limit the way that property or land can be used or developed. They are enforceable by landowners or leaseholders (where the property is divided into separate flats), against each other. Covenants are normally imposed to ensure that a development maintains a uniform appearance or to restrict the type of activities that can be carried out within a property. For example, they might forbid you from parking a caravan in the drive; or from displaying an advertisement or planting trees or hedges or erecting fences in the front garden. They might also prevent you from using the house for any other purposes than residential use. Some covenants require that you obtain approval for any proposed building works from the original estate developers, in addition to any planning permission or other consents that may be required.

Typically, such covenants are worded as:

> '. . . not to carry out any building works within the front part of your garden';

> '. . . not to display an advertisement or sign on any part of the property';

> '. . . not to use the property for any trade or business activity'; or

> '. . . not to park a caravan in your front drive'.

Once imposed, a covenant will be recorded on the title deeds of your home and will affect both existing and subsequent owners and occupiers of the house. Covenants apply to the house and are enforceable by the courts, not by your local council, and they can override any planning permission issued by the council. So, even if you have already obtained planning permission for certain works, you might be prevented from proceeding with the works because of a Restrictive Covenant.

To check if your home is subject to a Restrictive Covenant, look at the deeds of your house. Alternatively, some covenants may be recorded on the Land Registry entry.

If a breach of a covenant has occurred, then any beneficiary of the covenant (i.e. a neighbour or fellow resident) can apply to the courts for an injunction. If the injunction is granted, it will prevent the property owner in question from further breaching the covenant and could require the breach to be remedied, e.g. an unauthorised extension to be demolished. If the breach persists, then a claim for damages could follow. Remember that, while you can take action if your neighbours are in breach of any covenants, they can also take action against you if you were to breach the covenants. So, before planning or carrying out any works, it is important to identify whether your home or that of your neighbours is subject to Restrictive Covenants.

Covenants can only be removed or varied by applying to the Lands Tribunal under the terms of the *Law of Property Act* 1925. Once an application is received, the tribunal can discharge or modify the covenant on the grounds that it is obsolete; or because the persons benefiting from the covenant have, by act or omission, agreed to the discharge; or on the grounds that discharging or modifying the covenant will not result in any injury to the persons who benefit from the covenant.

Forms for applying to modify or discharge a Restrictive Covenant can be obtained from the Lands Tribunal at Procession House, 55 Ludgate Hill, London EC4M 7JW or from www.landstribunal.gov.uk. This website also contains general guidance on submitting applications and provides access to previous decisions of the Tribunal that may assist in understanding how applications are considered and reported.

⚠ Before planning or starting any works, check if your home – or your neighbour's – is subject to any Restrictive Covenants

Listed Building Consent

If your home is statutorily listed as a building of special architectural or historic interest, you may require a separate Listed Building Consent to carry out any alterations that affect the character of the building. This consent may be needed in addition to any planning permission, although in some situations it may be the only consent that you require.

You will require Listed Building Consent if you are proposing to demolish the building in whole or in part or want to carry out any internal or external alterations or extensions that would affect the special architectural or historic character of the building. Repairs will not normally require approval, unless they, too, involve alterations that will affect the special character of the building. Painting or redecorating a listed building may also require Listed Building Consent.

The control over works to a listed building extends to any object or structure fixed to the building or located within the grounds of the building and which has been there since before 1 July 1948. This is the concept of curtilage listing.

So, if you own or occupy a listed building, in addition to any necessary planning consents, you will need to obtain consent for works to both the interior and exterior and to any object or structure that is either attached to the building or located within the grounds and which has been there since before 1 July 1948.

Any application for Listed Building Consent must be made to your local council, following the same procedure as outlined in chapter 8 for a planning application. You can apply online by using the government's online planning service at www.planningportal.gov.uk or via your local council's website (see the council list at the back of the book). Prior to granting Listed Building Consent, the council has a legal obligation to consult English Heritage on the impact of your proposal on the listed building. If your application for Listed Building Consent is refused, you have the right of appeal and the appeals procedure is the same as that for planning appeals, which is described in chapter 9.

> ⚠ It is a criminal offence to demolish a listed building – either in total or in part – or to undertake any repair works that will affect its character without the prior consent of the council

> ⇨ More on planning appeals **chapter 9**

Conservation Area Consent

If your home is located within a conservation area, you will have to apply for Conservation Area Consent if you wish to demolish a building or to cut, top or lop a tree. Some exemptions apply to certain smaller buildings and trees. For instance, it is not necessary to obtain consent for the demolition of any building that does not exceed 115 cubic metres or to fell a tree that has a diameter of less than 7.5 centimetres when measured at a height of 1.5 metres above ground level. Consent is also not required to demolish a fence, wall or gate that is less than 1 metre in height if it adjoins a highway or public open space, or less than 2 metres in any other case.

Again, if your works require Conservation Area Consent, this must be obtained in addition to any necessary planning permission. For instance, if your home is located within a conservation area and you have obtained planning permission that allows the demolition of any part of your house, you will not be able to proceed with the works until you have obtained Conservation Area Consent for the demolition works.

> ⚠ Before undertaking demolition works in a conservation area, you must obtain Conservation Area Consent

Rights to Light

Your building work may interfere with the Rights to Light enjoyed by an adjoining property and, therefore, you may be open to action under the Rights to Light legislation. Rights to Light can be acquired in a number of ways, but generally there are two that are common. These are, firstly, rights that have been acquired by an express grant; and, secondly, those that are acquired by 20 years of uninterrupted enjoyment of natural daylight.

Rights to Light are civil matters that can only be actioned between immediate neighbours where their individual right to light is interfered with. The consequences of your carrying out building works that obstruct your neighbour's Rights to Light may result in action being pursued by your neighbour and a claim for compensation awarded by the courts.

> ⚠ If your building works obstruct your neighbour's Rights to Light, your neighbour may seek compensation through the courts

Access to neighbouring land

You may also have an obligation to ensure that rights of access to any neighbouring property are not interfered with. This obligation stems from the *Access to Neighbouring Land Act* 1992 and seeks to ensure that any persons who require access to neighbouring land for the purposes of carrying out any works are not prevented from doing so. For example, if you were to build an extension up to the site boundary, your neighbour might be prevented from gaining access to the adjoining part of their property and this could contravene the provisions of the above Act.

Wildlife

If you are proposing to demolish any existing buildings, fell trees or generally clear existing vegetation, or carry out any building works you may need to obtain a licence under the Wildlife and Countryside legislation if protected species or habitats will be disturbed. A variety of wildlife is protected under this legislation. This includes bats, nesting birds, reptiles, great crested newts, natterjack toads and badgers. It is generally an offence to disturb birds or birds' nests until the breeding season is over. Equally, bats and their habitats are protected and you cannot disturb these without first obtaining a licence. Surveys to detect the presence of protected wildlife and their habitats may be subject to seasonal constraints and, therefore, your project may have to be delayed to await the appropriate season when the survey can be undertaken.

Tree Preservation Order

If you wish to undertake any works to a tree that is subject to a Tree Preservation Order, you must submit an application to your local council. Applications can be made online at www.planningportal.gov.uk or via the council's website, using a standard application form, and you (or your tree surgeon or contractor) should provide information on the extent of the works that you are proposing and the reasons why. If the council refuses your application, you have a right of appeal to the secretary of state, as outlined in chapter 9. Appeals must be submitted within 28 days of the date of the council's decision.

You will not need the council's consent if you are proposing to cut down or prune a tree that is dying, dead or dangerous or which is directly in the way of a development that you are proceeding with under the terms of a detailed planning permission that has already been granted.

Have you covered everything?

You may have established that you do not need to obtain planning permission for your building works, but use the checklist overleaf as a handy reference guide to other consents or approvals that might be required.

Checklist of other matters to consider

Issue	Questions to consider	... And why?
Building Regulations	Is approval under the Building Regulations required?	If approval is required, make sure you obtain this before you start your building work, otherwise you run the risk of having a Building Regulations enforcement action served on you.
Party walls	Will the building work impact a party wall?	If the work will impact a party wall, you will need to serve a Party Wall Notice on the adjoining property owner.
Planning conditions	Are there any planning conditions imposed on the original planning permission for your home that restrict your Permitted Development rights?	If such conditions have been imposed, you must apply to the council for approval to undertake the works even if they would ordinarily be Permitted Development.
Restrictive Covenants	Are there any Restrictive Covenants that restrict the use or further development of your house?	If such a covenant exists, you will breach the covenant if you proceed with the works, even if you have obtained planning permission.
Listed Building Consent	Is your house listed?	If your house is listed, you may have to obtain Listed Building Consent before you can proceed with the building works, even if they do not need planning permission.
Conservation Area Consent	Is your home in a conservation area?	If your home is in a conservation area, you will have to obtain Conservation Area Consent if you want to carry out demolition works or to fell, lop or top trees.

THE DEVELOPMENT PROCESS – WHO DOES WHAT AND WHEN?

Rights to Light	Will your building works limit the natural light enjoyed by your neighbours?	If the works will limit your neighbours' natural light, you might interfere with their Rights to Light and at risk of their taking action against you.
Access to neighbouring land	Will your building works restrict access to your neighbour's house or will your access to the new building be restricted by them?	Remember that access to the neighbouring land can be secured by an order of the courts.
Wildlife	Will your building work involve the demolition of buildings or the removal of trees or vegetation?	If your works will involve such demolition works, this could result in damage or impact on species or their habitats that are protected and an offence will be committed if the proper licence has not been obtained or the work takes place at the wrong time of year.
Trees subject to a TPO	Will your work necessitate the cutting down, topping, lopping, or uprooting of a tree that is subject to a TPO?	If this is the case, you must get prior permission from the council.

The development process – who does what and when?

In order to continue with your development you may need to employ a building contractor who has access to a full team of specialists to cover the electrical, plumbing and services installations. Alternatively, you may decide to do some or all of the works yourself as a self-builder, although the electrical, plumbing and drainage services must be installed and certified by a specialist contractor. The 'Where can I find more information?' section at the back of the book will assist you in identifying sources of specialist help.

If you have already engaged the services of an architect or designer to prepare the drawings for submission to the council and to obtain tenders from the building contractor, it might be a good idea to retain the architect or designer to supervise the work and ensure that it complies with the drawings. If you are proceeding on the basis of Building Regulations approval only, the responsibility for ensuring that the works are carried out in accordance with the Building Regulations rests with the person you have appointed to undertake the building work.

When work has commenced and is in progress, you must ensure that the work is inspected for compliance with the Building Regulations at various critical and regular stages. There are two options available. You can either use an independent approved inspector or pay your local council to undertake the inspections and, ultimately, approve your building works.

Completion of the works

Once the works are completed, you should obtain a completion certificate from the council confirming that all the work complies with the Building Regulations. This is an invaluable certificate when selling your home.

What if the approved works are changed during construction?

It is not uncommon that, during the construction process, either you or your builder identifies some form of improvement that was not apparent at the design stage. For example, you may decide that an additional window

THE DEVELOPMENT PROCESS – WHO DOES WHAT AND WHEN?

would be useful or that the length of your extension should be increased to provide a little more space. There are risks associated with sanctioning additional works that have not been through the planning and Building Regulations approvals process.

Firstly, a breach of the Building Regulations may occur if the construction works are not proceeding in accordance with the regulations or in accordance with the plans that have been deposited with the council. Secondly, if the alteration results in a variation to the plans that were submitted when the Certificate of Proposed Lawful Development or Use was obtained, you could be at risk of prosecution for providing false or misleading information. Varying the plans could also alter the opinion that the works are Permitted Development and negate the certificate that the council issued.

Thirdly, the alteration may result in the development exceeding the Permitted Development threshold and bring it within the scope of the planning system. Although carrying out development without the requisite planning permission is not in itself an offence, the resulting development would be open to enforcement action by the council. Councils have various powers to pursue enforcement actions against any unauthorised development and these are described in chapter 10. If you are served with an Enforcement Notice, you have a right of appeal and this will result in the enforcement action being deferred until the appeal is determined, but the ultimate sanction is prosecution in the courts.

⚠ Make sure any works are carried out in accordance with the planning and Building Regulations or you risk being in breach of the regulations

⚠ If you change or vary the plans approved by the council without prior permission you could be prosecuted for providing false or misleading information

I DON'T NEED PLANNING PERMISSION

⚠️ Making unauthorised changes to the approved plans could take your works outside the Permitted Development thresholds and render your Certificate of Proposed Lawful Development or Use invalid

➡️ More on enforcement action that can be taken by the council **chapter 10**

Building – some golden rules
- Check if other consents are required
- If they are, make sure you obtain them and get written confirmation
- Stick to your plans
- Get consent if you want to change anything
- Seek help when you are beyond your knowledge zone

8 So I need permission – what now?

If you've established that you need to obtain planning permission for your works, you will now have to begin the process of preparing a planning application and submitting it to the council.

Applying for planning permission

You can submit planning applications either in outline or in full. For homeowner developments, a full application is usually the best option. This means that you or your architect will need to prepare full details of what is proposed, including elevations, sections and floor plans. It's often a good idea to seek professional help in preparing and submitting the application. If you choose to do this and the application is submitted in your agent's name, the council will send all correspondence to the agent and not to you as the applicant.

For larger-scale developments, it's often more appropriate to submit an outline application first. The purpose of an outline application is to establish that the principle of a development is acceptable before you commit to the detailed design stage. If you decide to apply in outline, you will still need to provide information on:

- the proposed use;
- the size of the development;

- a layout plan showing where you propose to extend the house;
- the upper and lower height, width and length of the proposed building; and
- where the access points to the site are to be located.

You can submit an outline application that reserves some details for approval at a later date. These are commonly referred to as the Reserved Matters and include:

- layout of the development in relation to the site and surroundings;
- scale of the building in terms of height, width and length;
- appearance of the building;
- access to the site and the building for pedestrians, cyclists and cars; and
- landscaping – how the space around the proposed building is to be landscaped both in terms of new planting, hard surfaces and screening.

Although one or more of the above matters can be reserved for subsequent approval, councils have powers to request further information where they consider that the information submitted is inadequate for a decision to be made.

Pre-application discussions with the council

Once you have put together your ideas and are almost ready to submit the planning application, it is useful to discuss the proposals with the council's planning officers and this is called a pre-application discussion. The practice varies between councils. Some councils charge for pre-application meetings. Other councils offer a consultation process before a planning application is submitted where they will give an opinion on the likelihood of the development proposals being granted permission and advice on any changes that could increase the prospects of its success.

Check with your council to see if it provides a pre-application consultation and advisory service, whether a charge is involved and how long it takes. Although the nature of the building works that you, as a homeowner, are proposing are unlikely to be contentious in planning terms, it is useful to obtain confirmation that this is indeed the case before formally submitting your application.

Pre-application discussions with your neighbours

It is also helpful at this stage to let your neighbours know that you are intending to submit a planning application for the building works at your home. This avoids any unwelcome surprise on their part when they receive the council's official notification letter letting them know that your planning application has been submitted.

By sharing your proposals with your neighbours beforehand, you may be able to take into account their objections. They might suggest some amendments that would make the proposal more acceptable to them and you could then consider these before committing to the planning application. This will increase the likelihood of your application proceeding more smoothly and could speed up the decision-making process.

What information should I include on an outline planning application?

You (or your appointed agent) will need to submit all of the information in the following list.

Other information	In an outline application, you are required to provide information on the proposed use; the amount of development that you are proposing; how the site will be laid out, the upper and lower limits of the proposed building in terms of height, width and length and where access is to be located.	✔
Reserved Matters	You must clearly indicate which matters you are applying for and those that you are reserving for subsequent approval. Reserved Matters can be any or all of the following: • layout; • scale; • appearance; • access; and • landscaping.	✔
Supporting information	Although this is not obligatory, you may provide further information in support of your application. You could, for example, state that you have discussed the proposal with your neighbours and they do not have any objections. You could also include details of any pre-application discussions you have held with the council's planning officers and how you have responded to any comments they made.	?

What information should I include on a full planning application?

When applying for full planning permission, you (or your appointed agent) will need to complete and provide the information on the following checklist.

WHAT INFORMATION SHOULD I INCLUDE?

Full application checklist		
Item to be included	**Things to consider**	
Householder application form	Make sure it is complete, duly signed and dated.	✓
Certificate of ownership	There are four possible certificates that you can use. If you are the owner of the property or if you hold a lease which has more than seven years to run, you will need to use certificate A. If you are not the owner, use certificate B, which confirms who the owner is and that you have given them notice that you are making a planning application. In the unlikely event that you do not know the names and addresses of the owners of the house, then use certificates C or D. The certificates are included in the planning application form.	✓
Agricultural holding certificate	This certificate confirms that no part of your house or garden forms part of an agricultural holding (see glossary) or, if it does, that you have served notice on any tenants that occupy any part of the holding. The certificate is included in the planning application form.	✓
Site location plan	The plan will usually be on a scale of 1:1250 or 1:2500 and should clearly identify your house and garden by reference to two named roads. Your home and garden should be identified in red and any other land that you control in blue. In practice, it is unlikely that you will have control over any other land that will need to be highlighted in blue. The plan should contain a north point.	✓

SO I NEED PERMISSION – WHAT NOW?

Site layout/block plan	This plan shows how your proposal relates to the existing house and the boundaries of your garden. It will be usually be on a scale of 1:500 or 1:200. The plan should contain a north point	✓
Floor and roof plans	You must submit both existing and proposed floor and roof plans and these should be on a scale of 1:50 or 1:100.	✓
Elevations	You should submit both existing and proposed elevations on a scale of 1:50 or 1:100. Elevations should be clearly marked 'east', 'west', etc.	✓
Sections	Submit existing and proposed sections through the building. These should be on a scale of 1:50 or 1:100.	✓
Application fee	Currently this stands at £150 for applications involving the enlargement, improvement or alteration of a dwelling or for operations and the erection of buildings within the curtilage of a dwelling. Payment of the fee is required at the time that you submit the application. No VAT is chargeable on application fees. There is no provision for a refund of the fee even if ultimately you withdraw your application or it is rejected. However, you will be entitled to a 'free-go' if you resubmit a further application following refusal of permission and the development proposed is of the same character or description on the same site. Application fees are regularly reviewed and increases are made from time to time, so check with the council. In the unfortunate event that your cheque is dishonoured, the processing of your application will cease.	✓

Design and Access Statement	You will only need to submit a Design and Access Statement if your home is located within a conservation area, an Area of Outstanding Natural Beauty, National Park, a World Heritage site, the Broads or within a Site of Special Scientific Interest (see glossary).	?
Supporting information	Although this is not obligatory, you may provide further information in support of your application. You could, for example, state that you have discussed the proposal with your neighbours and they do not have any objections. You could also provide details of any pre-application discussions you have held with the council's planning officers and indicate how you have responded to any comments they made.	?

Submitting your application

You should submit your planning application to your local council. The information to be included in your planning application is based on a nationally agreed list. However, councils have the power to add specific local requirements, so check your council's website for any specific additional application requirements for householder developments. If you discuss your proposal with the council's planning officers beforehand, ask what information they will need to register and process the application or call the planning department and confirm the requirements over the phone.

You must attach three copies of all drawings and supporting documents, plus the original – four in total. Always keep a copy of the application and any supporting documents and drawings for your own reference or, if you have appointed an agent to handle the submission, ask for a copy of all the submitted documents and drawings. Some councils ask for additional copies of the application to assist in their consultation process, although this usually only happens in the case of major development proposals. Again, you can check this with the council's planning officers if you have a pre-application meeting.

Design and Access Statements

In the case of a householder planning application, you will only need to include a Design and Access Statement if your property is located within a designated area, such as a conservation area, an Area of Outstanding Natural Beauty, a National Park, a World Heritage site, the Broads or within a Site of Special Scientific Interest. If this is the case, the statement must be included in both an outline and a full planning application. Where Listed Building Consent is required and a Design and Access Statement is also needed, a single Design and Access Statement can be used for both the planning and listed building applications. A Design and Access Statement is not required in applications for Advertisement Consent.

The Design and Access Statement should explain how you have considered your development in the context of the site and surroundings; what options you have thought about and what design and access principles (amount of development, layout, scale, landscaping and appearance of the building) you have taken into account and adopted. It should also identify what access options for pedestrians, cyclists and cars you have considered and any consultations (with the council or neighbours) that you have undertaken.

Environmental Impact Assessment

There is a remote possibility that the development you are proposing will require an Environmental Impact Assessment (EIA). This is most unlikely, because this

SUBMITTING YOUR APPLICATION

procedure is designed to assess major development proposals in environmentally sensitive areas where there may be potentially significant environmental effects. Should an EIA be required, though, it must be submitted with the planning application. In the event of any doubt, you can apply to the council for a Screening Opinion to determine whether or not your proposed works require an EIA, but make sure you do this before you submit your planning application.

To apply for a Screening Opinion, write to the council and enclose:

- a plan sufficient to identify your land;
- a brief description of what you are proposing and the possible effects on the environment; and
- any other information that you think would help the council to form an opinion.

The council has a statutory obligation to let you know its response within three weeks, although it may request an extension of the time period. You have a right of appeal to the secretary of state if the council fails to respond to your letter or you disagree with the council's decision.

Will I need extra help?

For an outline application, the only drawings that are required are a location plan and a site layout or block plan and you should be able to prepare these without assistance. The location plan will normally be based on an ordnance survey plan, which can be obtained from an ordnance survey or other web-based map provider. Details of these are provided at the back of the book under 'Where can I find more information?'.

To prepare the type of drawings that are required to accompany a full application, however, you will require

SO I NEED PERMISSION – WHAT NOW?

Councils have powers to decline to deal with applications that are the same, or substantially the same, as a previous application that has been dismissed on appeal within the previous two years. Such powers also extend to applications that have not been subject to an appeal but where there have been at least two refusals within the past two years. These powers are designed to avoid a succession of applications aimed at wearing down the council's resistance to a development proposal. So, when contemplating any building work at your home, it is important to consider the previous planning history of the house and to check if there are any failed attempts in the past that could jeopardise your plans.

⚠ Your application must include all the required documents, drawings and the application fee or it will not be validated

⚠ If your cheque is dishonoured, your application will cease to be processed

⚠ Check the planning history of your house – if a previous planning application has been refused within the previous two years, your application could be declined

How your application is processed

If you apply online, you should receive an electronic response confirming receipt and assigning a reference number to your application. For all documents sent by post or submitted online, the council will firstly check the submitted material and, if satisfied, will proceed to formally register the application. This process can take between three and five days. Once validation and registration is complete, the application is entered on the planning register and a unique reference number assigned by the council. An acknowledgment letter will be sent to you (or your appointed agent) confirming that the application is registered and giving the reference number and the name of the officer at the council who will be dealing with it. If you do not hear anything from the council within five days,

SUBMITTING YOUR APPLICATION

call them to check that your application has been received and when you can expect to receive the formal acknowledgment letter.

The formal acknowledgement letter will confirm the target date for reaching a decision. For minor applications involving extensions and alterations to individual dwellings, this will be eight weeks from registration. If the council wishes to go beyond the eight-week determination period, it must obtain your consent to do so but, most importantly for you, it will provide you with a right of appeal to the secretary of state on the grounds that your application has not been determined within the target date. Whether you decide to exercise your right of appeal or not depends on the reason why the application is taking so long to be determined, the reaction to the development proposals from the planning officer and whether a favourable decision is imminent. Appealing on the grounds of non-determination will take the application out of the council's hands and place it within the jurisdiction of the Planning Inspectorate and this will, on average, add a further 16–19 weeks to the process if the appeal is processed by written representations and longer for appeals by informal hearing or inquiry (see chapter 9).

Once the application is validated and registered, the council will instigate a consultation process that involves sending details of the application to statutory consultees, e.g. the highway authority, water authority, the local parish or town council and, in the case of applications for Listed Building Consent, etc., English Heritage, and asking them for comments. The council may advertise the application in the local press or at the application site and will notify your neighbours that an application has been received and that the details can be inspected on its website or at the council offices. Some councils ask applicants to display a site notice at the application site confirming that a planning application has been submitted. The nature and scope of notification of planning applications received

SO I NEED PERMISSION – WHAT NOW?

varies between councils, but will involve both consultation with statutory organisations and notifying local residents, including your immediate neighbours, and inviting their comments.

Statutory consultees and local residents will be given a deadline to submit comments in writing to the council either by post or online. This will be either 14 or 21 days from the day when details of the application are circulated. A period of 14 days is normally adopted where the notice of the planning application is published in the local newspaper. In practice, many statutory consultees seek an extension of time and, in the case of local residents and statutory consultees, councils frequently accept comments beyond the stipulated time period. However, your council cannot legally make a decision on the application until the 21-day statutory time period has expired.

Officers from the council will visit the site to assess the development proposals in the context of the site and its surroundings. Armed with the results from the site visit and any comments received from the consultation process, they will take a view on the proposal. Principally, they will assess the development in the context of the policies contained within the Local Development Plan. They may request further information in order to complete their assessment or suggest that modifications or amendments are made to the proposal that could make it more acceptable. Such requests will be communicated to either yourself or your agent. In this instance, you may have to commission and submit revised drawings and this will result in some form of re-consultation usually over a more limited time period.

The decision-making process

Your planning application will be determined either by the planning officers or by council members sitting on a planning or development control committee. Applications determined by planning officers are done so under powers of delegation, which means that the council has formally delegated power to its officers to take decisions on certain planning applications. The extent of powers that are delegated to officers varies between councils, but such powers are clearly defined and will usually relate to applications that have attracted few or no objections, that accord with the development plan and that are supported by the officers. In some cases, officers have delegated powers to refuse applications. Council members may also ask for a specific application to be brought before a committee for determination. Objections from neighbours will invariably serve as a trigger for determination by a committee or attract interest amongst councillors who then ask for the application to be heard at committee. That is why it is advisable for you to discuss your proposals with your neighbours before submitting the planning application and to keep in contact with them during the application process in order to reduce the risk of objectors railroading or delaying your plans. There is increasing pressure from government to make more and more planning applications subject to decisions by officers under delegated powers, particularly for the type of minor developments frequently proposed by homeowners, so this is likely to become more commonplace in future.

If your application proceeds under delegated powers, the council's planning officers will have the authority to make the decision.

Councils are under increasing pressure to determine planning applications within the statutory time period of eight weeks in the case of minor applications. A minor application comprises a proposal for nine or less dwellings or a building less than 1,000 square metres. This pressure is generated by a link between councils' performance and their qualification for government grants. So, if the council asks you for further information, or requests any amendments, you should aim to respond quickly. If you don't, there is a risk that the council will proceed to determine the application without waiting for your response and this will invariably end up with a refusal of permission. If you do submit amendments, the council may re-consult on the changes and this could result in your application extending beyond the eight-week determination target. While you may be happy to accept this, the council will not and they may try to persuade you to withdraw the application and resubmit with the amendments included. Where delegated powers are available to the council's planning officers, a decision can be made almost at will once the statutory consultation process has been completed. It is vital that you or your agent maintain regular contact with the case officer throughout the application process and avoid being 'pressurised' to withdraw, or you may face a refusal at the point where the eight-week determination period is about to lapse.

If your application is to be presented to the council's planning committee for determination, you will be notified of the time and date and of any rights you have to address the committee before it makes a decision. The committee meeting will also be open to the public. The officer will be required to prepare a report and present the application to the committee, and the agenda and reports for consideration by the committee will be published usually five working days before the meeting. At this stage they will become public documents and you will be able to obtain a copy either by accessing the council's website or by visiting the council offices. It is important that either you or your agent obtain a copy of the officer's report because it will confirm how the application is viewed, what the officer's recommendation is and the nature of any objections that have been submitted by your neighbours or any statutory consultees. If your application is recommended for refusal, the five days' publication date provides you with an important opportunity to address any concerns directly with officers, neighbours and committee

THE DECISION-MAKING PROCESS

members. Leaving it this late in the process, though, should be viewed as a last resort, primarily because it may be difficult to overturn an officer's recommendation. Your best chances are to canvass support from your local councillors and persuade your neighbours to withdraw their objections.

Not all councils allow objectors or applicants to address the planning committee. If your council does allow this, you should take advantage of this opportunity, particularly if the application is recommended for refusal. Any address to the committee will be restricted to between three and five minutes, depending on your council's adopted policy. This opportunity will also be extended to those persons who wish to object to the development and they will be able to speak for the same period. Your neighbours may therefore turn up on the night to address the committee about their concerns. Some councils allow committee and local members to ask questions of both the applicant and objectors. Following any presentation by objectors, applicants and by the council officers, the committee will proceed to consider the application and make a decision. This could be to accept the officer's recommendation, reject it or defer a decision pending further information or a site visit. In the latter instance, the officers will report back to a future meeting of the planning committee. The committee's decision will be final, although any decision may be subject to an appeal, as described in chapter 9, or a challenge to the High Court.

⚠ Maintain regular contact with the case officer and respond quickly to requests for further information – otherwise the council may proceed to determine your application without this in order to hit the eight-week target and you could end up with a refusal

⇨ Challenging a planning decision **page 118**

Section 106 agreements

In a small number of cases, the council may indicate that it is content to grant permission for your development proposal but, before doing so, requires you to enter into an agreement with them that regulates the development in some way. Such an agreement is prepared under the powers of section 106 of the 1990 Act and is referred to as a 'section 106 agreement'. It would be unusual, but not inconceivable, for a section 106 agreement to be imposed on a householder application. For example, the council may require you to restrict the use of a proposed building in your garden to one that is ancillary to your house rather than as a separate dwelling. So, you might be able to move granny into the annexe in your garden with the proviso that the annexe did not become a separate dwelling to your home. Or the council may require you to demolish an existing extension before you are allowed to build a new one. Some councils also insist on a one-off financial contribution from anyone undertaking a development that will create new bedspaces, in order to offset the increased demand on the local infrastructure. Financial contributions can only be secured by a section 106 agreement.

If a section 106 agreement *is* required, this will be evident from the planning committee report, or the planning officers may have already identified the need for one, and the agreement must be signed before any planning permission can be issued. You will require the assistance of your solicitor to draft the agreement and ensure that your legal obligations are safeguarded.

A simpler alternative is for you to make a formal commitment to the council to fulfil any obligation by means of a written undertaking. This is called a 'unilateral undertaking'. It is similar to a section 106 agreement, but only your signature is required.

Should your development proposal generate the need for any form of agreement, you should obtain legal advice as to which is the best option for you.

THE DECISION-MAKING PROCESS

Agreements made under section 106, and those where the terms of the agreement have a lasting effect, are legally binding on successors in title. For example, if you are obligated to maintain a granny annexe as ancillary to the main house, this will be registered as a land charge against your property and will apply to all future owners of the property. But where an agreement requires you, for example, to make a contribution towards local infrastructure, once the contribution has been made, the terms of the agreement will have been fulfilled and have no lasting effect for subsequent owners.

Withdrawing your application

You can withdraw your application at any point before it is determined by the council. All you have to do is write to the council confirming this. The council will then take no further action on the application and it will be entered as 'withdrawn' on the planning register. Usually, you would only consider withdrawing your application if it seemed that the council were proposing to refuse it. For instance, the council may have suggested that, with some amendment, your proposal would be supported, in which case it is best to resubmit your application with the suggested amendments incorporated. Withdrawing the application is preferable to receiving a refusal of permission, because a refusal will be entered on the planning register and appear every time a search is made. Alternatively, it may be that you have submitted a planning application for a house you were hoping to purchase and the sale has fallen through. Withdrawal of the application in these circumstances is also appropriate.

If you withdraw your application, the application fee will not be refunded. However, you will be entitled to a free-go when you resubmit, providing you do this within 12 months of the date when you submitted the earlier application and the proposal is substantively the same. You are only entitled to one free-go.

SO I NEED PERMISSION - WHAT NOW?

Applying - some golden rules
- Consult your council and your neighbours first
- Seek professional or technical assistance at an early stage
- Make sure your application is complete
- Keep in touch with the case officer
- Monitor the progress of the application on a regular basis
- Utilise any rights to address the planning committee

The planning decision

Once a decision on your application has been made by either the council's planning committee or by the council's officers, you will receive a formal decision notice. This is a legally binding document. If the planning committee made the decision, you will already be aware of the outcome because either you or your agent will have attended the committee meeting.

So, now you will either be the proud owner of a planning permission or a disappointed recipient of a planning refusal. Whatever the result, it is important that you carefully consider the decision notice.

Even if planning permission has been refused, the decision notice might suggest that, with some amendment, your proposal could be acceptable. Alternatively, you have the option of challenging the refusal.

On the other hand, although planning permission may have been granted, it may contain a number of conditions that you will need to comply with.

⚠ Read the decision notice carefully - a planning permission may have conditions attached, or a refusal might suggest your proposal could be acceptable with certain amendments

⇨ More on planning appeals **chapter 9**

THE PLANNING DECISION

Planning conditions

Councils have broad powers to impose conditions as they generally see fit. However, in practice, government guidelines and interpretation by the courts has given rise to a discipline requiring that conditions are only imposed if they meet all of the following tests. A condition must be:

- necessary for the purposes of allowing the development to proceed;
- relevant to the purposes and function of the planning system;
- fair and reasonable in relation to the development to be permitted;
- enforceable by the council in terms of practicality and ability;
- sufficiently precise for the applicant to understand what is required and when; and
- not unduly restrictive and be reasonable in all other respects.

You may not be happy with some of these conditions and you have a right to appeal against any that you consider are onerous or excessive. However, before you decide to lodge an appeal against a specific condition, bear in mind that the inspector will consider the whole permission again and could decide to change conditions that you have not appealed against, or to insert more conditions or refuse permission. In such a situation, it is advisable to submit an application to the council seeking to modify or vary the condition that you find unacceptable and then, if that application is refused, to appeal against this decision. In this way, your planning permission will not be interfered with.

There may be other conditions that require you to submit further information to the council for approval before you commence any works on site. It is important to follow the requirements of these conditions closely because a failure to do so can nullify the permission. So, for example, if the condition requires that samples of the materials to be used in the construction of the external surfaces of the approved extension shall be submitted and approved in writing by the council before you commence the works, then you must do this. If you fail to do so, the council has powers to issue a Breach of Condition Notice and there is no right of appeal against such a notice.

The permission will be subject to a standard time limit. In the case of a full planning permission, the development must be commenced within three years from the date of the permission. For an outline permission, the Reserved Matters will have to be submitted for approval within three years and the development commenced within two years of the final approval of the Reserved Matters, whichever is the later. Councils do have powers to vary the time limits within which permissions must be implemented, although it is unlikely that they will exercise these powers in the case of minor development projects.

Your planning permission comprises not just the formal decision letter but also the drawings and information that you submitted with it. The decision notice may list the drawings that have been approved; if it doesn't, you will have to check the drawings that formed part of your application. Your permission must be implemented only in accordance with these approved drawings.

If the permission expires before development is commenced, you will have to reapply with a fresh planning application and this will be judged on the basis of the planning policies applicable at that time. You must not assume that permission will automatically be renewed, so it's essential to keep a close eye on the expiry date if you are not ready to proceed immediately on receipt of the permission.

⚠ Think carefully before appealing against a specific condition – the whole permission will be reviewed again and other conditions might be changed or added or the whole permission refused

⚠ If you proceed with your works, you must abide by any planning conditions or the council could issue a Breach of Condition Notice, against which there is no appeal

⚠ If you fail to start work before the permission expires, don't assume that a fresh planning application will automatically be granted

⇨ More about a Breach of Condition Notice **page 141**

Discharging conditions

Before you proceed with your development, or during the course of your building work, it is important to fulfil any conditions that have been imposed on the planning permission at the appropriate time, i.e. prior to commencement of the works or before the building is occupied. This process is called 'discharging conditions'. You should obtain written approval that you have done so and keep copies for your own records.

⚠ Make sure you get written approval from the council of any conditions you have discharged

Implementing your permission

You can commence your development by undertaking what is known as a material operation. This can include any work of construction in the course of erecting the development, such as:

- the digging of a trench to contain the foundations or part of the foundation of the building;
- the laying of any underground main or pipe to the foundations or part of the foundations or to the trench that will contain the foundations;
- any operation in the course of laying out or constructing a road or part of the road; or

SO I NEED PERMISSION – WHAT NOW?

- any change in the use of the land that constitutes material development.

Once development has been commenced in accordance with the planning permission, the permission will remain in perpetuity, and no further permission will need to be obtained for these particular works. However, before you proceed with any works, you must ensure that any conditions imposed on the planning permission have been discharged where they required approval of details to be obtained prior to work commencing.

Amending the approved drawings

Occasionally, you may want to make some amendments to the approved drawings. If you do decide to depart from these drawings, you must obtain approval from the council.

Some amendments may be so minor that the council's planning officers are able to accept them as minor modifications, although it is important to obtain written confirmation of this. Other changes may be viewed as major and you may be asked to submit a fresh planning application and have to start the planning application process again.

New powers introduced in the 2008 Act will allow councils to accept changes to a planning permission, providing they are satisfied that the change is not material. This will avoid the need to reapply for planning permission. When exercising these powers, though, councils will be able to impose new conditions or vary those that they originally imposed on the planning permission.

Challenging a planning decision

Before you start work, there is one final point to bear in mind. All decisions of the council can be subject to judicial review. Any person who is aggrieved by the council's decision can seek judicial review. So, for example, your neighbour could seek a judicial review on the planning permission that you have obtained. However, they would only be able to do this on the grounds that there was a legal defect in the way the application was processed or in the way in which the permission is drafted. For example, it is not enough for a neighbour merely to be upset by the decision or the fact that the council did not give sufficient weight to their objections.

Applications for a judicial review of a planning decision should be submitted to the courts within three months of the date of the planning decision. Claimants seeking a judicial review will be expected to have sufficient interest in the matter and will probably already have lodged objections during the planning application stage. It will therefore be evident in the lead up to the determination of your application whether your neighbour or somebody in the locality is so vehemently opposed to your proposal that, should they not achieve the desired outcome from the council, might be prepared to go to the next level to sustain their objection. Applications for a judicial review of the permission that are submitted after the three-month period will not be accepted. For further information on making a High Court challenge, visit www.courtsservice.gov.uk or write to: Administrative Court, Royal Courts of Justice, Queens Bench Division, Strand, London WC2 2LL.

⚠ All council planning decisions can be subject to judicial review

Ready to go? Some final checks

If you have received your permission and are confident that your neighbours are not so unhappy that they will apply to the courts to reverse the decision, you can get ready to start your works. There are two final checks to

SO I NEED PERMISSION – WHAT NOW?

make. Firstly, ensure that all pre-commencement conditions are satisfactorily discharged. Secondly, before you instruct the builder to start on site, take another look at the checklist in chapter 7 and make sure that you have applied for and obtained any other consents or approvals that are required, e.g. Building Regulations approval or party wall agreements.

Implementing – some golden rules
- Before starting, make sure all pre-commencement conditions are discharged
- Discharge any other conditions at the appropriate time
- Check you have obtained any other consents or approvals
- Stick to your approved plans
- If you wish to vary the plans, get approval first
- Take care that your permission does not expire
- Keep records of any further approvals obtained, particularly those confirming that conditions have been complied with

9 They said no! What do I do?

Can I reapply?

If your planning application has been refused, you may feel the planning process has let you down, but you don't necessarily have to abandon your plans completely. It may be that the reasons given for refusal of permission and the way the council has justified its decision suggest that if you amend your proposal in some way, the objections could be overcome. For example, the refusal may be based on an unacceptable level of overlooking of your neighbour's house by the inclusion of new windows in your planned works. A redesign that either omits the offending windows or replaces a clear glass window with obscure glass may be sufficient to overcome the council's objection, in which case it's worth resubmitting the application with these changes included.

So, when you receive the refusal notice, your first task is to study closely the reasons for refusal and consider whether the objections can be overcome in a way that still provides the additional accommodation or other solution that you require. You may wish to obtain professional or technical advice on whether a resubmission of your application is feasible. If you (or your adviser) decide to go ahead with this, then you will have to restart the planning application process, including the pre-application discussions with your council and neighbours, as outlined in chapter 8. Any reapplication will need to demonstrate how the council's objections have been overcome, because the council has powers to decline to deal with 'repeat' planning applications.

⚠ When making a fresh planning submission, you will have to go through the whole application process again

⇨ More on council powers to decline to deal with 'repeat' submissions **page 105**

Can I appeal against the decision?

If you decide that amending the proposals in order to overcome the council's objections would be too restrictive, you have a right of appeal against the council's decision. This right of appeal applies whether your planning application has been refused or the council has failed to determine it within the statutory time period. You can also appeal against conditions that have been imposed on a planning permission if you consider that they are unacceptable or unreasonable. There is nothing to stop you from reapplying *and* submitting an appeal at the same time, although one course of action could prejudice the other. For example, a council faced with a resubmitted planning application *and* an appeal may simply refuse planning permission again on the grounds that an appeal is live. And, if your second planning application is refused, this could strengthen the council's case at appeal.

The appeals process is administered by the Planning Inspectorate and an inspector will be appointed to deal with your appeal. The inspector will be independent of the council who determined the planning application.

How are appeals processed?

Appeals must be lodged within six months of the council's decision on your planning application or the date when the council should have made its decision, i.e. the target date

CAN I APPEAL AGAINST THE DECISION?

set out in the acknowledgment letter sent to you when your application was first submitted, as described in chapter 8.

There are three options for pursuing appeals. The first option is based on **written representations** and involves an exchange of written statements between you and the council and then a site visit by the inspector. The second option initially involves the preparation and submission of written statements, followed by a discussion of the merits of the proposal in front of the inspector at an **informal hearing** and then a site visit. The hearing is conducted informally and chaired by the inspector. The third option involves the exchange of written statements, followed by an inquiry where oral evidence is presented by all parties to the appeal which is then subject to examination by the opposing party at a **public inquiry**. A site visit then follows. Of all three options, the public inquiry is the most formal and potentially the most expensive. The informal hearing option is less formal, but still requires the convening of a hearing, which will take some time to set up, while the written representations option represents the least expensive and the quickest of the appeal options. The written representations procedure is usually the most suitable option for householder developments because it is likely to be less controversial and is capable of assessment on the basis of the exchange of written evidence and a site visit, although in practice it has the lowest success rate. Which option you select will generally reflect the range of issues that need to be considered.

Currently, approximately 80 per cent of all appeals are processed by written representations, 16 per cent by informal hearings and 4 per cent by public inquiry. Of all appeals, approximately one-third are successful, with the success rate being greatest for appeals processed by public inquiry, then by informal hearing and, lastly, by written representations.

THEY SAID NO! WHAT DO I DO?

The average timescales for determining appeals varies. Appeals processed by written representations will take on average 20 weeks, while those subject to an informal hearing will take 30 weeks and those by public inquiry between 18 and 30 weeks.

Whether or not you decide to appeal, and indeed which appeal route you pursue, requires careful consideration. While, in general, the costs of any appeal are borne by the parties to the appeal, in the case of appeals processed by informal hearing or public inquiry, you, as the appellant, have the opportunity to apply for costs against the council. On the other hand, the council can also seek an award of costs against you! An award of costs is usually associated with unreasonable behaviour on the part of either the council or the appellant, or a failure to provide sufficient proof of why planning permission should, or should not be granted. The late withdrawal of an appeal could count as unreasonable behaviour and result in costs being awarded against you. So, think very carefully when deciding whether to opt for an informal hearing or public inquiry and make sure that you will not be exposed to any costs being claimed against you because you have not provided sufficient support for each ground of your appeal. An award of costs does not automatically follow the appeal decision. So, for example, you could win the appeal, but still have an award of costs against you for a delay in submitting appeal documents.

At the time of going to press, the government was considering introducing the option of costs in respect of appeals processed by the written representations method and it is therefore likely that these will be introduced during 2009.

When deciding whether or not to appeal, you should review the reasons for the refusal of the planning application thoroughly; or the reasons why a particular condition has been imposed or why the council has not determined the application within the target date. Appeals, like applications, are determined in accordance with the provisions of the Local Development Plan unless there are material circumstances that dictate otherwise. Give some thought as to whether the council's reasons for refusal could be contested and principally why you consider that permission should be granted, with regard to the planning policies in the development plan.

If you decide to go ahead, you will need to decide which option is most suitable for progressing the appeal. As a general rule, it is likely that the written representations option is most appropriate for householder developments, unless the proposal has been rejected on subjective grounds, such as the design is not in keeping with the local area, and you don't agree with this. In this instance, you may decide that arguing your case in front of the inspector at a hearing will provide you with a better chance of success. Alternatively, if, say, the proposal for your new garage has been refused because the council incorrectly claims that there is insufficient room for a car to access it, then this is a matter of fact and easier to deal with by the written representations option.

Although you may elect for an appeal to be heard at a hearing, the Planning Inspectorate may decide that a hearing is not justified on the basis of the case submitted and try to encourage you to revert to the written process. The Inspectorate's view is that an appeal is suitable for the written representations method if:

- it is not for an agricultural worker's dwelling or similar that is dependent on demonstrating a business need and financial viability;
- there is evidence that neither the council nor the appellant wish to claim costs;
- it is possible to argue and understand the appeal on the basis of written submissions, photographs and a site visit; and

- there is no need to hear evidence under oath or cross-examine witnesses.

Powers have recently been introduced under the terms of the 2008 Planning Act that restrict the ability of appellants to select which appeal option they favour. Instead, the Planning Inspectorate will have the power to determine how the appeal should be progressed irrespective of any preferences selected by either you or the council. At the time of writing this book, these new powers had not yet been brought into effect.

A fast-track householder appeals system is currently being piloted in a number of council areas. It is likely that this will be adopted nationally by secondary legislation in April 2009. The fast-track appeals system is based on the council submitting only the application case file and internal documents electronically and the appellant providing their full grounds of appeal at the time of submitting the appeal. No further written exchanges are permitted from the council, appellant or any third parties and unless you need to attend the site to allow the inspector to gain access he or she will carry out an unaccompanied site visit. The pilot scheme has reduced average appeal processing times to 12 weeks. The system of appeals by householders is therefore likely to become even more streamlined and quicker once the pilot scheme is adopted nationally.

⚠ To avoid an award of costs against you in an appeal processed by an informal hearing or a public inquiry, make sure you provide sufficient support for each ground of your appeal

What information do I need to submit my appeal?

Having decided that a case can be made and made the decision to appeal, you can now start to prepare and submit the appeal. It is important to stick to the six

WHAT INFORMATION DO I NEED TO SUBMIT MY APPEAL?

months' timetable and to ensure that the Planning Inspectorate receives all appeal documents within six months of the council's decision. Late appeals are only accepted in exceptional circumstances.

The appeal documents you need to prepare are:

- the appeal form duly signed and completed (the form can be accessed online at www.planning-inspectorate.gov.uk);
- the relevant land ownership certificate confirming that you were the owner of the site prior to the appeal being submitted;
- a copy of the planning application that you submitted to the council;
- a copy of the land ownership certificate that you submitted with the planning application;
- a list, and copies, of all drawings, documents and plans that comprised the planning application and which were submitted to the council, including any supplementary information submitted during the processing of the application, and the Design and Access Statement if one was required;
- a copy of any Environmental Impact Assessment or Screening Opinion issued by the council, if you submitted one with your application. In practice, because of the relatively small scale of your building work, it is most unlikely that you will require an EIA and so you will probably not have had reason to ask the council for a Screening Opinion (see page 103);
- copies of any correspondence submitted to or exchanged with the council during the application process;
- the council's decision notice (if you are appealing against refusal or conditions imposed);

127

- a plan showing the site in relation to two named and established roads, with the site marked in red; and
- if a Reserved Matters decision, a copy of the original outline planning permission and supporting plan.

The appeal, with the above documentation, should be submitted to: The Planning Inspectorate, Temple Quay House, 2 The Square, Temple Quay, Bristol, BS1 6PN.

Appeals can be made online on the Planning Inspectorate's website (www.planning-inspectorate.gov.uk).

Send a copy of the appeal form to the council, together with copies of any new documents or drawings that were not submitted with your planning application. In the case of written representation appeals, the appeal documentation should include your full grounds of appeal. For appeals proceeding by hearing or public inquiry, an outline of the grounds of appeal is sufficient because you don't need to submit the full grounds of appeal until a later stage in the appeal process. Most importantly, keep a copy of all the appeal documents that you submit.

The 2008 Act has introduced powers to allow a fee to be introduced for submitting an appeal, but at the time of writing these had not yet been brought into effect.

⚠ Make sure you get your appeal in on time – late appeals are only accepted in exceptional circumstances

Can I do the appeal myself?

There is no reason why you cannot prepare and submit the appeal yourself, particularly if you have chosen the written representations option. However, you may require professional help, depending on the number and types of issues to be dealt with. If you elect for the appeal to be heard at a hearing or inquiry, you will need technical and professional support and this could be provided by an architect or planning consultant or, in the case of a public inquiry, a solicitor.

In any event, it is useful to obtain a professional view before you decide to appeal. This will help to clarify and confirm your chances of success and help you to decide which is the best appeal option to choose. It will also assist in identifying any additional technical assistance you need. For example, if your application for a new building has been rejected because there is inadequate visibility from a proposed access, then you may find it helpful to use the services of a highway engineer. Most importantly, a professional view will highlight any weak areas in your case that could result in costs being awarded against you if you were to proceed with your appeal on your own.

The appeal process

Once submitted, the appeal will be validated and registered by the Planning Inspectorate. A start date and unique appeal reference will be assigned. The start date is important because it determines the deadline for submission of statements and evidence. The appeal will then proceed in one of the following ways, depending on the option you have chosen.

Appeals by written representations

Within two weeks of the start date, the council will issue an appeal questionnaire, which will include copies of relevant correspondence, the planning officer's report to the committee, the relevant committee minutes and extracts from the development plan highlighting the policies that the council is relying on to defend its decision.

When submitting the appeal questionnaire, the council will indicate whether it is proposing to prepare an additional written statement or whether it will be relying only on the documents attached to the questionnaire. For appeals proceeding under the 'householder appeals pilot' scheme, the council will submit a copy of the original application file together with any internal reports and this will represent their written submission at this stage.

Within six weeks of the start date, you can submit any further comments on the appeal and the council can do the same.

Within nine weeks of the start date, you will have the opportunity to comment on the council's appeal documents and statements. Likewise, the council has the right to comment on your appeal documents. At this stage in the appeal process, there is only an opportunity to comment on the submissions made by other parties and no additional evidence can be introduced.

After nine weeks, neither party will have the opportunity to submit anything further in writing and the next stage is confirmation of the site visit by the inspector. The site visit can be accompanied or unaccompanied, depending on the feasibility of inspecting the site from the public highway. If an accompanied site visit is considered necessary, you or your representative will have to attend, together with a representative from the council. An accompanied site visit will not proceed if one of the parties to the appeal is not represented. The purpose of the site visit is for the inspector to inspect the site and surroundings and he or she will not engage in any discussion or listen to new evidence. The visit is a simply a familiarisation process to provide information for the determination of the appeal and no decision will be made at this visit. Instead, the inspector will end the site visit when satisfied that he or she has seen everything. The inspector may also visit neighbouring properties to assess the impact on your neighbours. Any concerns from your neighbours will already have been identified during the appeal process and the inspector will have already noted their interest.

THE APPEAL PROCESS

After the site visit, the inspector will write up the decision letter and a copy will be issued to you, to the council and to anyone else who has requested a copy. The decision notice will be issued within five weeks from the date of the site visit.

⚠ At the nine-week stage in the appeal process, each party can only comment on the submitted appeal documents and statements and no additional evidence can be introduced

Appeals by informal hearing

Appeals proceeding by an informal hearing are subject to the same two-, six- and nine-week written exchanges as for written representation appeals. The main written evidence will, however, be presented in the form of a hearing statement at the six-week stage and, therefore, there is no need when submitting your appeal to prepare a full statement of your grounds of appeal. Nevertheless, it will still be necessary to provide sufficient information to explain why you disagree with the council's decision with specific reference to each of the reasons for refusal outlined in the formal decision notice.

At the end of the written exchanges, i.e. nine weeks, a hearing will be convened and you will have an opportunity to discuss the case in front of the inspector in an informal forum before the hearing takes place. The council and any other persons with an interest in the outcome will be invited to attend and can address the inspector about their concerns. You will then be offered a date for the hearing. If this is inconvenient and you decline the date, the Planning Inspectorate will fix another date without offering you any choice in the matter. The hearing will usually take place at a venue provided by the council and will commence at 10 a.m. on the appointed day.

The hearing will be conducted in an informal manner with the inspector in the chair. The inspector will open the proceedings and explain the protocols for the hearing. He or she will have already identified the key issues from the written submissions. It is important therefore to ensure that your written submissions are expansive and fully record your concerns. The inspector will lead the discussion, allowing you, the council and any other interested persons to comment and contribute to the debate. Any neighbours who objected to your planning application could therefore attend and speak against the development. You may encourage your other neighbours to attend the hearing to speak in favour of your application, but in order for them to do so they must notify the Planning Inspectorate of their intent. The inspector will also invite discussion on conditions to assist in the decision-making process, although will make it clear that any such discussion is without prejudice to the final decision.

At the end of the hearing, the inspector will carry out a site visit. The process is similar to the written representations site visit, but depending on the inspector's guidance, evidence from all interested parties can be discussed at the site visit.

If you are proposing to apply for costs on grounds of the unreasonable behaviour of the council, the inspector will identify an appropriate moment in the proceedings and this will usually be at the end of the discussion. The council will also be invited to apply for costs if you have acted unreasonably in the appeal. Generally, however, both you and the council are normally expected to cover your own costs in the appeal. Guidance on what constitutes unreasonable behaviour is set out in government circular 8/93 'Awards of costs incurred in planning and other (including compulsory purchase order) proceedings'. Examples of unreasonable behaviour that might prompt an award of costs are the late withdrawal of the appeal either after the exchange of all the written evidence or just prior to the hearing taking place. A failure to provide sufficient information to back up one of the grounds of appeal may also constitute unreasonable behaviour. For example, it might be that you submit your appeal on the grounds that the development complies with the planning policies in the development plan, only to find on closer scrutiny that it does not. If you persist with this argument and cause the council to undertake work that then proves to be fruitless, they may seek costs against you. Although it's fairly uncommon for costs to be awarded, you should nevertheless consider the implications when preparing your appeal.

After the hearing, the inspector will write up the decision and a copy will be sent to you, to the council and to any interested party who attended the hearing and requested a copy. The target date for decision letters to be issued is within seven weeks of the hearing.

⚠ Unreasonable behaviour that could result in an award of costs is late withdrawal of the appeal, e.g. after the written exchanges, or failing to provide sufficient evidence to support any one of the grounds of appeal

Appeals by public inquiry

Appeals by public inquiry follow the same timetable and process as written representation and informal hearing appeals up to the nine-week stage.

After nine weeks, a public inquiry will be convened and four weeks prior to the commencement of the inquiry you will be required to submit a statement of the evidence that you intend to present at the inquiry. The council are obligated to do likewise. These statements, referred to as 'proofs of evidence', will be subject to oral examination at the inquiry. They should be based on, and expand on, the statements of evidence that were produced at the six-week stage. At least four weeks prior to the inquiry commencing, you will also be expected to produce a statement of common ground that identifies the matters where you and the council are in agreement. The statement should be agreed and signed by both you and the council and then submitted to the Planning Inspectorate.

The inquiry will take place at a time and place confirmed by the Planning Inspectorate. You will be entitled to decline only one offer of an inquiry date. After that, the Inspectorate will impose an inquiry date. The council will normally provide the venue and the proceedings will commence at 10 a.m.

The public inquiry is more formal than the informal hearing and, although chaired and managed by the inspector, it proceeds along similar lines to a court hearing, with 'witnesses' presenting their evidence and then being subject to 'cross-examination'. Discussion on conditions will be invited in the same way as for informal hearings and any applications for costs will be heard at the end of the inquiry, before the site visit takes place.

At the closure of the inquiry, the inspector will arrange a site visit. The site visit follows a similar format to appeals by written representations and informal hearings but, subject to the inspector's discretion, evidence may be heard from either side on site.

After the inquiry, the inspector will write up the decision and send a decision letter to you, to the council and to any other interested party who attended the inquiry and requested a copy. The target date for issuing the decision letter is seven weeks from the close of the inquiry. In a very limited number of appeals, usually those associated with major developments of a controversial nature, the inspector will submit the decision letter to the secretary of state who is then responsible for issuing their own decision.

Submitting appeal documents

During the appeal process, you should submit all documents directly to the Planning Inspectorate in

THE APPEAL PROCESS

duplicate. The Planning Inspectorate has the responsibility for distributing a copy of the documents to the council and to any other parties. Appeal documents can be submitted online on www.planning-inspectorate.gov.uk. It is important to ensure that documents are submitted to the Planning Inspectorate within the stipulated timeframes.

⚠ Late submissions will not be accepted and will not feature in the appeal proceedings

Householder appeals service (HAS)

The current householder appeals pilot scheme is likely to be rolled out and applied throughout England during the course of 2009. The key advantages and requirements of this scheme are outlined below.

The council will rely on its application case file and any existing internal reports to defend its position, rather than producing a specific appeal statement, and will not attend the site visit.

The appellant will send their appeal statement with the appeal form and only attend the site visit if it is necessary for the purposes of providing access.

On the basis of this streamlined process, the average processing time is expected to reduce from 12 weeks to eight weeks. Written representation appeals are at present averaging 16 weeks and those utilising the householder pilot scheme 12 weeks.

How long will my appeal take?

From the start date, all written exchanges for appeals by written representations and informal hearings will be concluded within nine weeks. For appeals proceeding by public inquiry, the exchange of evidence and a statement of common ground will be required four weeks prior to the commencement of the inquiry.

The target date for site visits in appeals by written representations is 12 weeks from the start date. For appeals held by informal hearing or public inquiry, the target dates for completion are between 20 and 28 weeks from the start date.

Following the site visit, the target time for a decision letter to be issued is five weeks in the case of written representation appeals, seven weeks for informal hearings and also for public inquiries which last for one or two days. From start to finish therefore the average appeal times are as follows:

- 20 weeks for written representation appeals;
- 30 weeks for appeals by informal hearing; and
- 18–30 weeks for appeals by public inquiry.

The appeal decision

At the end of the appeal process, the inspector's decision letter will be posted to you or, if you requested an electronic copy, it will be e-mailed to you. In this letter, the inspector will set out why your appeal should either be dismissed or upheld. If the appeal is upheld, this letter will constitute the planning permission and any conditions deemed appropriate will be listed. You can then proceed to implement the permission in exactly the same way as if you had received the permission from the council. However, your obligation to discharge conditions in accordance with the stated timescales and to obtain any other consents or approvals remains the same. If the appeal is dismissed, the decision letter will set out the reasons why planning permission should not be granted.

Almost all decisions are the responsibility of the individual inspector. In a small number of appeals, the inspector reports to the secretary of state who is then responsible for issuing the decision. However, this only usually happens for appeals concerning major or more controversial development proposals and it is unlikely that the secretary of state will intervene in developments proposed by homeowners.

⇨ More on discharging conditions **page 117**

⇨ More on other consents and approvals **chapter 7**

> **Appealing – some golden rules**
> - Submit your appeal in time – if late you will lose your right to appeal
> - Think carefully about which method to use
> - If you withdraw, do it early to avoid an application for costs against you in appeals by hearing or inquiry
> - Make sure you can substantiate your appeal or you may be liable to costs against you in appeals by hearing or inquiry
> - Submit all the information when required to do so
> - Follow the appeal timetable – late submissions will be returned

Challenging the appeal decision

If the outcome of the appeal is not what you were hoping for, then your options are limited. It may be that in rejecting an appeal, the inspector has suggested that, with some amendment or adjustment, the proposals would have been acceptable. In such situations, you could submit a revised planning application to the council and should succeed in obtaining planning permission.

If you have any questions or complaints about the way the appeal was processed, you have the option of requesting the Planning Inspectorate to investigate. However, the appeal will not be reopened or reconsidered and the outcome will merely be a conclusion as to whether the complaint is justified or not. Complaints can be submitted to the Quality Assurance Unit at the Planning Inspectorate (e-mail: complaints@pins.gsi.gov.uk).

Alternatively, all appeal decisions can be challenged by making an application to the High Court. A challenge will only be successful if it is shown that the inspector made an error in law in making the decision. A successful challenge will result in the appeal being reconsidered, but there is no guarantee that the outcome will be any different. An appeal to the High Court must be made within six weeks of the date of the original appeal decision.

⇨ More on making a revised planning application **page 121**

⇨ Challenging a planning decision **pages 118–119**

10 Why don't I just start work without planning permission?

As you navigate your way through the complexities of the planning process, you may very well ask yourself why you don't simply start work without planning permission. Perhaps you have already received a refusal of planning permission and failed to persuade an inspector on appeal that permission is justified. Or maybe you are about to embark on what seems a long and winding road through the planning system and are considering whether the end justifies the means.

Strangely, the act of undertaking development work without first applying for planning permission is not a criminal offence in itself. The offence is committed when you fail to comply with an Enforcement Notice issued by the council that requires you to take steps to remedy the breach. The powers of the council to take action against unauthorised development are extensive but, most importantly, they are discretionary.

Before taking any enforcement action against an unauthorised development, the council must firstly consider whether it is expedient to do so. To a large extent, expediency is contingent on the nature of the breach, the impact that it has on the amenity of those living nearby and whether, if a planning application were actually submitted, the council would have granted permission and imposed conditions that could effectively exercise some control over the unauthorised development in an acceptable manner.

Enforcement tools

If you have carried out some form of development without first applying for planning permission, you may be faced with all or some of the following enforcement 'tools' at the council's disposal.

- **Planning Contravention Notice** – a notice served by the council to obtain information about the development that has taken place and to establish legal interests in the property. This is usually a precursor to enforcement action, but does not apply to breaches involving listed buildings, conservation areas or trees that are subject to preservation orders as, in such instances, the council's remedy is to prosecute directly through the courts.

- **Enforcement Notice** – a notice that requires the specified breach of planning control to cease within a defined time period. There is a right of appeal against an Enforcement Notice and, once an appeal is submitted, the notice is held in abeyance until the appeal is determined. Appeals against an Enforcement Notice proceed in much the same way as those involving a refusal of planning permission as described in chapter 9. Appeals must, however, be lodged before the date when the notice takes effect. This date will be clearly stated on the notice.

- **Stop Notice** – a notice that will require a specified activity to cease immediately. There is no right of appeal against a Stop Notice and it will have immediate effect. A Stop Notice can only be served once a related Enforcement Notice has taken effect.

- **Temporary Stop Notice** – a notice that can be issued requiring the unauthorised activity to stop immediately. The council can issue a Temporary Stop Notice without first issuing an Enforcement Notice.

The effect of the notice is immediate and you have no right of appeal. However, its provisions are temporary.

- **Breach of Condition Notice** – a notice which identifies that a condition imposed on a planning permission has been breached. You do not have any right of appeal against a Breach of Condition Notice and once it has taken effect you are liable to prosecution in the magistrates' court. The powers of the council to issue a Breach of Condition Notice renders it imperative that you seek to discharge any conditions imposed on a planning permission in the appropriate manner as described in chapter 8.

⚠ Appeals against an Enforcement Notice must be lodged before the date when the notices takes effect

⚠ Make sure you discharge any planning conditions in the appropriate manner or within the stated timescale, or the council could issue a Breach of Condition Notice, against which there is no appeal

Buildings of architectural interest

If your home is a listed building, be aware that it is a criminal offence to demolish the building in whole or in part and to carry out any works of alteration or extension that affect the character of the building. This applies to both internal and external works. Councils have powers to serve a Listed Building Enforcement Notice, against which there is a right of appeal in much the same way as a normal Enforcement Notice. However, there are also further powers for councils to serve a Building Preservation Notice where a building that is not listed, but is considered to be of potential architectural or historical interest, is threatened with demolition or alteration. If you receive such a notice, it will take immediate effect and will remain in force for six months while the Department for Culture, Media and Sport (DCMS) considers whether the building should be added to the statutory list.

WHY DON'T I JUST START WORK?

If your home is not listed but still of some architectural or historic value, there is a further device that is available to the DCMS if you are proceeding with either demolition or alterations that could threaten the character of the building. Applications can be made for the building to be 'spot listed'. The department will then consider the application and decide whether to add the building to the statutory list.

⚠ It is a criminal offence to demolish the whole or part of a listed building without the prior consent of the council or to undertake internal or external works that affect its character

Impact on neighbours

You should be alert to the sensitivity that your building work may have in your neighbourhood. Although the scale of what you are doing may be relatively small and, in your opinion, unlikely to cause offence, your neighbour may take a different view. A window that creates overlooking or increases the perception of overlooking may be significant to your neighbour and prompt them to call the council's enforcement team and ask them to investigate your building work. Once the complaint has been logged, the council will be obligated to investigate, although it may not necessarily decide to take action.

⚠ Think about the impact that your building work could have in your neighbourhood – it might seem insignificant to you, but not to your neighbour

Unauthorised developments

Even in the light of the council's legal powers to deal with unauthorised developments, you may have decided to proceed with the building works regardless. Alternatively, you may have purchased a house and inherited some form of unauthorised development that was undertaken by a previous owner. If an extension or alteration has been built

UNAUTHORISED DEVELOPMENTS

without planning permission, is substantially completed and has remained in place for four years without the council taking any action against it, then you can apply for a Certificate of Lawful Development to confirm that it is lawful. This also applies if a change of use has occurred to a building or part of a building to use as a single dwelling and the use has continued for four years without any enforcement action being taken. Once the time limit has passed, then the use becomes lawful.

An application for a Certificate of Lawful Use is made in a similar manner to an ordinary planning application, although the information to be submitted is different. In the case of an application for a Certificate of Lawful Use or Development, the onus is on the applicant to provide evidence that a use has continued for a period of four years or that the building was substantially completed four years before the date of the application. Once the council has granted a certificate, it cannot pursue enforcement action against the use or development that is referred to in the certificate. It is an offence to provide false or misleading information in support of an application and the council has powers to revoke a certificate if it is found that their decision was based on false or misleading information.

⚠ Providing false or misleading information in support of an application for a Certificate of Lawful Use or Development is an offence and could result in the council revoking the certificate

11 How do I stop neighbouring developments?

If you are contemplating any development works that could impact your neighbours, it's advisable to let them know before formally applying for planning permission. Likewise, you may receive a similar approach from your neighbours if they, too, are proposing to undertake development at their home. However, it may be that the first you know about your neighbour's proposal is when a notification letter from your local council arrives through your letterbox. This letter will notify you that a planning application has been received and that you can inspect the proposals either at the council offices or online via the council's website.

The letter will further advise you that you can make representations for or against the proposal and that, if you do, you should do so in writing and submit them to the council within a prescribed timescale, which is usually 21 days. The practice of notifying neighbours that a planning application for an adjoining or neighbouring property has been received varies amongst councils and some rely on notices displayed at the application site rather than sending out notification letters. Others display a notice in a local newspaper confirming the planning applications that they have received.

Keeping track of development activity by your neighbours requires you to be proactive and to be familiar with the notification processes used by your local council. It is useful to contact your council and establish what methods they use and, thereafter, to monitor these so you can identify any planning application activity that could affect your home at the earliest opportunity. This, of course, applies not just to development proposals by your neighbours but all development activity within your area.

Your neighbours may simply start their building work without obtaining planning permission. Or it may be that the work they are planning is allowed under Permitted Development, so 'bricks and blocks' arriving next door may not always signal that something illegal is taking place. If you have any concerns or suspicions, contact your neighbours first and, if their response is unsatisfactory, get in touch with the council. Councils have dedicated enforcement teams who deal with and investigate complaints into unauthorised development activity, so direct your complaints to this department in the first instance. Bear in mind that the council will probably ask for your name and address and 'confidential' complaints are not normally encouraged. So it is likely that your neighbour will soon find out that you have complained. The council will investigate your complaint and let you know the outcome. This may confirm that the building work is unauthorised or that it is Permitted Development. If the work is unauthorised, then the council will advise you of what action it proposes to take.

How to review what your neighbours are proposing

Once you have identified that your neighbours are proposing to carry out a development that requires planning permission, it is important to inspect the plans. You could approach your neighbours to request a set of the drawings, but once a planning application has been submitted, it becomes a public record and so it may be more convenient for you to inspect the copy held by the council.

HOW DO I STOP NEIGHBOURING DEVELOPMENTS?

The crucial task is to assess what is proposed and how it could impact on your property. So, study the drawings in relation to your property – how far away from the boundary will the development be and what height, and will there be additional windows that could overlook your garden? Planning seeks to regulate development activity in the public interest and, therefore, private matters are irrelevant when determining a planning application. So, for instance, the impact on property values or the personal circumstances of the applicant are not material planning considerations. Also, no one has an automatic right to a view, so the critical question is: will the proposal have an unacceptable impact on the amenity of your property?

When assessing the plans, focus on matters that are relevant to planning. If you bring up non-planning matters, this can dilute the importance of any legitimate planning objections. For example, will the development result in an unacceptable loss of daylight or sunlight from that which you currently enjoy? Will there be increased overlooking of your garden as a result of the development proceeding? Or could it adversely impact trees in your garden on account of the proximity of the proposed building to the boundary? Will there be an unacceptable increase in parking on adjoining streets or will the resulting development obscure visibility from an existing access point? Will the proposal result in detriment to your amenity as a result of increased smells, noise, disturbance or nuisance? These issues are not intended to be exhaustive and, in practice, there is no clear dividing line between planning and non-planning considerations.

Having identified your concerns, you may decide to pursue these directly with your neighbours. However, it is important to submit your concerns in writing to the council to ensure that they are duly logged as objections within the stated timescale.

⚠ Any objections to neighbouring developments should be made in writing to the council within the stipulated deadline

How to object to your neighbours' proposals

The council's notification letter will set out how, where and when to submit your comments. Most councils accept objections by e-mail, but your objective is to ensure that your objections are submitted in writing and within the prescribed timeframe. Although the notification letter may indicate that you should submit your objections by a specified date, in practice councils will accept late letters. However, it's best not to rely on this, so always aim to submit your letter by the stipulated date.

Many councils do not acknowledge receipt of objections. Nor do they automatically re-consult when proposals are amended in response to objections. So you must maintain contact with the planning case officer at the council who is responsible for handling the application in order to obtain updates on the application's progress. The initial notification letter will usually give the name of the case officer and will contain an application reference number that you should quote on all correspondence. Depending on the nature of your objections, you may also wish to send copies of any correspondence to the local elected council members to ensure that they are aware of your concerns. If you do not know who your local councillors are, you can find their details on the council's website.

Your local parish or town council will be consulted on the planning application and invited to submit comments to the council. Although they have no powers to enforce a particular decision, their comments are invariably influential in the consultation process. Meetings of the parish council are often open to the public and it's a good idea to inform your local parish or town councillors of your concerns, because they may choose to oppose the development for similar reasons.

In your letter of objection, try to translate your concerns into valid planning objections, for instance by identifying any conflict with planning policies. Remember, the council's objective will be to initially test the proposals against planning policies in the development plan and, therefore, any policy conflict that you can highlight will assist in their assessment.

Maintaining a dialogue with the planning case officer is important, and you should do the same with your neighbour as this could help to reconcile your concerns in an amicable way. Also, by making contact with fellow neighbours, you may also find that your concerns are shared by others and a coordinated approach to objections and representations is then possible.

Any representations that are submitted in writing will become a public document and, therefore, accessible to your neighbours. So make sure your representations are worded so as not to cause offence!

⚠ Make sure the council receives your letter of objection by the stipulated date to ensure it is taken into consideration

What happens next?

At the end of the consultation period, the planning application will proceed in a number of ways. If your objections (and those of your fellow neighbours) are accepted by the council, the application may be refused or the applicant may be invited to submit amended proposals to overcome the objections. Alternatively, your objections may be rejected and the council will issue a planning permission.

Decisions, whether approval or refusal, can be taken by the council's planning officers under delegated powers, as outlined in chapter 8. The extent of officer-delegated powers varies amongst councils. So, at an early stage in your dialogue with the council, check the scope of the officers' delegated powers to approve or refuse planning applications.

WHAT HAPPENS NEXT?

Alternatively, the application may proceed to be determined by the council's planning committee, which is made up of elected councillors, and they will receive a report and recommendation from their officers. They will ultimately be responsible for determining the application and are not obligated to accept the officers' recommendation, although they will need sound planning reasons to go against a recommendation from their professional advisers. Your local ward councillor may sit on the planning committee and it is always advisable to channel any contact to council members initially through this person. He or she will advise you of the protocols for ensuring that other planning committee members are aware of your concerns and objections. You may wish to invite them to your property to witness for themselves the potential impact that the neighbouring development will have.

A number of councils have now adopted a practice whereby applicants and objectors can address the committee prior to a decision being made. There is usually a time limit on how long you are allowed to speak for, but it presents a further opportunity to highlight any outstanding concerns that have not been addressed during the application process or in the officer's report. If you and your fellow neighbours are all objecting, it will be necessary to coordinate your objections and nominate one person to represent all the views of the local community. Applicants or their agents will also have the opportunity to address the planning committee. When addressing the committee, again make sure your concerns are based on planning grounds.

Once a decision has been taken either by council officers or elected members, it is legally binding unless overturned on appeal or challenged in the High Court. So, if planning permission is granted and your objections have not been taken into account, the only recourse is to apply for judicial review in the High Court (see chapter 9). However,

HOW DO I STOP NEIGHBOURING DEVELOPMENTS?

you can only exercise this option when the legality or validity of the decision is in doubt. You will also have to demonstrate that you have sufficient interest in the matter and this will be easier to prove if you were an objector at the application stage.

Remember that whether or not your neighbour requires or has obtained planning permission, they may still need to obtain any other consents or approvals and these may provide a number of options for challenging what your neighbours are proposing even if they have successfully secured planning permission or it has been established that their building works are Permitted Development (see chapter 7).

If the planning application is rejected, your neighbour may elect to appeal against the decision. If an appeal is pursued, you, as an objector, will be notified by the council of the receipt of an appeal and invited to submit representations directly to the Planning Inspectorate. If the appeal proceeds to an informal hearing or public inquiry, then you will also have the opportunity to attend in order to present your concerns and observe the proceedings. There is no right of appeal available to objectors and so you will not be able to appeal against the council's decision.

Finally, if you remain aggrieved about the way that the council has handled the planning application and considered your comments, you can refer the matter to the local government ombudsman (www.lgo.org.uk). However, the ombudsman will not be able to investigate a complaint about the decision itself, only about the way the council handled the planning application.

⇨ More on delegated powers to council planning officers for determining planning decisions **page 109**

⇨ Other consents or approvals that might be needed **page 77**

ACCESS TO PUBLIC INFORMATION

> **Objecting – some golden rules**
> - Talk to your neighbours to see if your concerns can be overcome
> - Submit your objections in writing and within the stated deadline
> - Share your concerns with your local parish and district councillors and seek their support
> - Keep in contact with the case officer to find out how the application is progressing and when and how it will be determined
> - Join forces with your fellow residents to add weight to your objections
> - Attend the planning committee meeting to speak against the proposal if possible
> - Make sure your objections are based on planning grounds
> - If your neighbour obtains planning permission, check that they also obtain any other consents or approvals that are relevant

Access to public information

The *Freedom of Information Act* 2000 allows access to information held by or on behalf of public authorities. This means that you are able to view reports prepared by your council on planning applications and to inspect the background files that have been used in preparing any reports. Committee reports become public documents usually five working days prior to the committee meeting. Once the committee papers are published, the planning application case file will be available for inspection as a background document to the committee report. Some councils make the application file available earlier and it is important to check your local council's practice in these matters.

You can formally apply to the council for information under the terms of the 2000 Act, if you do not receive the

HOW DO I STOP NEIGHBOURING DEVELOPMENTS?

information that you requested beforehand. If you are dissatisfied with the council's response or consider that information has been withheld, you can make a complaint to the council. If you consider that your complaint has not been resolved, then recourse is available to the Information Commissioner's Office (ICO) at www.ico.gov.uk or write to: Information Commissioner's Office, Wycliffe House, Water Lane, Wilmslow, Cheshire, SK9 5AF.

Councils are also obligated to keep a public register of all planning applications and the decisions that are made. This is a useful record to check for any pending applications or the outcome on previous applications. The method of maintaining the register varies between councils. Some are held in paper format, some on microfilm and others in electronic format. A check with the council's planning administration section will determine how the planning register is kept and how it can be inspected.

⇨ List of planning authorities in England and Wales **page 155**

Summary checklist

The following is a checklist to help you ensure that your neighbours' development proposals do not adversely impact your home and garden.

SUMMARY CHECKLIST

How to stop neighbouring developments	
Step	**Activity**
1	Once you become aware of the proposed development, obtain plans and thoroughly review the proposals and consider how they will impact your property.
2	Immediately raise any concerns with your neighbours (or their agent).
3	Contact your local council to establish how and when planning application files can be accessed and to confirm their procedures for processing planning applications by officers or committee.
4	If your concerns are not resolved, submit formal objections (on planning grounds) to your local council.
5	Send copies of your objections to the local parish or town councillors.
6	Contact your local parish or town councillors to ensure that they are aware of your concerns and attend their meeting when the application is considered.
7	Send copies of your objections to your local ward councillors and, subject to their advice, to other members of the planning committee.
8	Contact the council's case officer who is dealing with the application to confirm firstly that they have received your objections and then whether or not they agree with your concerns and how and when the application will proceed to determination.
9	Contact your fellow neighbours to establish whether they are equally concerned and whether a combined objection or petition would be appropriate.
10	Maintain contact with the case officer, ward councillors and planning committee members to ensure that you are aware when the application will be considered and whether it will be supported or opposed.
11	Arrange to inspect the planning application case file to establish what other representations may have been submitted opposing the development proposal.

HOW DO I STOP NEIGHBOURING DEVELOPMENTS?

12	If officers are going to determine the application themselves, press your local councillors to request that it is determined at committee.
13	If the application proceeds to planning committee, obtain and review the committee report.
14	Register for the opportunity to address the planning committee.
15	Liaise with your fellow neighbours to ensure that the opportunity to address the committee is maximised.
16	Keep in contact with your local ward councillors and planning committee members in the lead up to the meeting to ensure that they do not forget your concerns.
17	Attend the planning committee meeting to monitor the discussion and address the meeting.
18	At this stage, your efforts will have been rewarded with a refusal of planning permission or you will have to take stock of the way the application was processed and determined and consider whether there is any ground for a complaint to the ombudsman or a challenge to the High Court.

List of planning authorities in England and Wales

Name of council	Address & contact details
ENGLAND	
Adur District Council	Planning Services, Civic Centre, Ham Road, Shoreham-by-Sea, West Sussex, BN43 6PR; Tel: 01273 263239; www.adur.gov.uk
Allerdale Borough Council	Planning Services, Allerdale House, Workington, Cumbria, CA14 3YJ; Tel: 01900 326418; www.allerdale.gov.uk
Alnwick District Council	Environment and Regeneration Department, Allerburn House, Denwick Lane, Alnwick, NE66 1YY; Tel: 01665 510505; www.alnwick.gov.uk
Amber Valley Borough Council	PO Box 18, Development Division, Town Hall, Ripley, DE5 3SZ; Tel: 01773 570222; www.ambervalley.gov.uk
Arun District Council	Planning Services, The Arun Civic Centre, Maltravers Road, Littlehampton, BN17 5LF; Tel: 01903 737500; www.arun.gov.uk

LIST OF PLANNING AUTHORITIES IN ENGLAND AND WALES

Ashfield District Council	Development Control Section, Council Offices, Urban Road, Kirkby in Ashfield NG17 8DA; Tel: 01623 457355; www.ashfield-dc.gov.uk
Ashford Borough Council	Planning and Development, Civic Centre, Tannery Lane, Ashford, Kent, TN23 1PL; Tel: 01233 330264; www.ashford.gov.uk
Aylesbury Vale District Council	Planning Department, 66 High Street, Aylesbury, HP20 1SD; Tel: 01296 585858; www.aylesburyvaledc.gov.uk
Babergh District Council	Babergh Planning, Control Division, Council Offices, Corks Lane, Hadleigh, IP7 6SJ; Tel: 01473 822801; www.barbergh.gov.uk
Barnsley Metropolitan Borough Council	Planning and Transportation Services, Development Control Section, Town Hall, Barnsley, S70 2TA; Tel: 01266 770770; www.barnsley.gov.uk
Barrow-in-Furness Borough Council	Town Hall, Duke Street, Barrow-in-Furness, LA14 2LD; Tel: 01229 894269; www.barrowbc.gov.uk
Basildon District Council	St Martin's Square, Basildon, SS14 1DL; Tel: 01268 533333; www.basildon.gov.uk
Basingstoke and Deane Borough Council	Planning and Development Services, Civic Offices, London Road, Basingstoke, Hants, RG21 4AH; Tel: 01256 845453; www.basingstoke.gov.uk
Bassetlaw District Council	Planning Services, Queen's Buildings, Potter Street, Worksop, S80 2AH; Tel: 01909 533418; www.bassetlaw.gov.uk
Bath & North East Somerset Council	Planning Services, Trimbridge House, Trim Street, Bath, BA1 2DP; Tel: 01255 477627; www.bathnes.gov.uk
Bedford Borough Council	Planning Services, Room A111, Town Hall, St Paul's Square, Bedford, MK40 1SJ; Tel: 01234 221720; www.bedford.gov.uk
Berwick-upon-Tweed Borough Council	Council Offices, Wallace Green, Berwick Upon Tweed, Northumberland, TD15 1ED; Tel: 01289 301847; www.berwick-upon-tweed.gov.uk

LIST OF PLANNING AUTHORITIES IN ENGLAND AND WALES

Birmingham City Council	Planning Control Division, PO Box 28, Alpha Tower, Suffolk Street, Queensway, Birmingham, B1 1TU; Tel: 0121 303 1115; www.birmingham.gov.uk
Blaby District Council	Desford Road, Narborough, Leicester, LE19 2EP; Tel: 0116 275 0555; www.blaby.gov.uk
Blackburn with Darwen Borough Council	Planning Section, Regeneration Department, Town Hall, Blackburn, BB1 7DY; Tel: 01254 585960; www.blackburn.gov.uk
Blackpool Borough Council	Customer First Centre, Municipal Building, Corporation Street, Blackpool, FY1 1NF; Tel: 01253 476229; www.blackpool.gov.uk
Blyth Valley Borough Council	Planning and Environmental Protection Department, Council Offices, Avenue Road, Seaton Delavel, Whitley Bay, NE25 0DX; Tel: 01670 542288; www.blythvalley.gov.uk
Bolsover District Council	Planning Services, Sherwood Lodge, Bolsover, Chesterfield, S44 6NF; Tel: 01246 242243; www.bolsover.gov.uk
Bolton Metropolitan Borough Council	Planning Control Section, Room 315, 3rd Floor, Town Hall, Bolton, BL1 1RU; Tel: 01204 336000; www.bolton.gov.uk
Boston Borough Council	Planning Department, Municipal Buildings, West Street, Boston, PE21 8QR; Tel: 01205 314345; www.boston.gov.uk
Bournemouth Borough Council	Planning and Development Services, Environment and Community Services Directorate, Town Hall Annexe, St Stephens Road, Bournemouth, BH2 6EA; Tel: 01202 451228; www.bournemouth.gov.uk
Bracknell Forest Borough Council	Time Square, Market Street, Bracknell, RG12 1JD; Tel: 01344 351400; www.bracknell-forest.gov.uk
Bradford Metropolitan District Council	Development Services, 3rd Floor South, Jacobs Well, Bradford, BD1 5RW; Tel: 01274 434195; www.bradford.gov.uk/planning

LIST OF PLANNING AUTHORITIES IN ENGLAND AND WALES

Braintree District Council	Causeway House, Bocking End, Braintree, CM7 9HB; Tel: 01376 551414; www.braintree.gov.uk
Breckland District Council	Elizabeth House, Walpole Loke, Dereham, NR19 1EE; Tel: 01362 656245; www.breckland.gov.uk
Brentwood Borough Council	Planning Services Department, Town Hall, Ingrave Road, Brentwood, CM15 8AY; Tel: 01277 261111; www.brentwood-council.gov.uk
Bridgnorth District Council	Westgate, Bridgnorth, WV16 5AA; Tel: 01746 713100; www.bridgnorth-dc.gov.uk
Brighton and Hove Council	Development Control Team, Environmental Services, Hove Town Hall, Norton Road, Hove, BN3 3BQ; Tel: 01273 292191; www.brighton-hove.gov.uk
Bristol City Council	Environment, Transport and Leisure, 1st Floor, Brunel House, St Georges Road, Bristol, BS1 5UY; Tel: 0117 922 3097; www.bristol-city.gov.uk
Broadland District Council	Planning Control Department, Thorpe Lodge, 1 Yarmouth Road, Thorpe St Andrew, Norwich, NR7 0DU; Tel: 01603 430615; www.broadland.gov.uk
Bromsgrove District Council	Planning and Development Department, Council Offices, Burcot Lane, Bromsgrove, B60 1AA; Tel: 01527 881330; bromsgrove.whub.org.uk
Broxbourne Borough Council	Development Control Department, Bishops' College Churchgate, Cheshunt, Hertfordshire, EN8 9XQ; Tel: 01992 785510; www.broxbourne.gov.uk
Broxtowe Borough Council	Planning and Community Development, Council Offices, Foster Avenue, Beeston, NG9 1AB; Tel: 0115 917 7777; www.broxtowe.gov.uk

LIST OF PLANNING AUTHORITIES IN ENGLAND AND WALES

Burnley Borough Council	Planning Services Department, PO Box 29, Parker Lane, Burnley, BB11 2DT; Tel: 01282 425011; www.burnley.gov.uk
Bury Metropolitan Borough Council	Environment and Development Services Department, Craig House, 5 Bank Street, Bury, BL9 0DN; Tel: 0161 253 5287; www.bury.gov.uk
Calderdale Borough Council	Planning Services, 2nd Floor, Northgate House, Northgate, Halifax, HX1 1UN; Tel: 01422 392237; www.calderdale.gov.uk
Cambridge City Council	Environment and Planning Department, The Guildhall, Cambridge, CB2 3QJ; Tel: 01223 457103; www.cambridge.gov.uk
Cannock Chase Council	Planning Control, Civic Centre, PO Box 28, Beechcroft Road, Cannock, WS11 1BG; Tel: 01543 464521; www.cannockchasedc.gov.uk
Canterbury City Council	Development Control and Planning Department, Military Road, Canterbury, CT1 1YW; Tel: 01227 862176; www.canterbury.gov.uk
Caradon District Council	Luxstowe House, Liskeard, Cornwall, PL14 3DZ; Tel: 01579 341404; www.caradon.gov.uk
Carlisle City Council	Planning Services, The Civic Centre, 6th Floor, Rickergate, Carlisle, CA3 8QG; Tel: 01228 817000; www.carlisle.gov.uk
Carrick District Council	Development Services, Carrick House, Pydar Street, Truro, Cornwall, TR1 1EB; Tel: 01872 224502; www.carrick.gov.uk
Castle Morpeth Borough Council	Environmental Protection Unit, Council Offices, The Kylins, Morpeth, NE61 2EQ; Tel: 01670 535087; www.castlemorpeth.gov.uk
Castle Point Borough Council	Planning Department, Council Offices, Kiln Road, Benfleet, SS7 1TF; Tel: 01268 882283; www.castlepoint.gov.uk
Charnwood Borough Council	Development Control Services, Southfields, Southfields Road, Loughborough, LW11 2TN; Tel: 01509 263151; www.charnwoodbc.gov.uk

LIST OF PLANNING AUTHORITIES IN ENGLAND AND WALES

Chelmsford Borough Council	Development Management, PO BOX 7544, Civic Centre, Duke Street, Chelmsford, CM1 1XP; Tel: 01245 606 826; www.chelmsfordbc.gov.uk
Cheltenham Borough Council	Built Environment Development Control, PO BOX 12, Municipal Offices, Cheltenham, GL50 1PP; Tel: 01242 264328; www.cheltenham.gov.uk
Cherwell District Council	Planning and Development, Bodicote House, Bodicote, Banbury, OX15 4AA; Tel: 01295 252535; www. cherwell-dc.gov.uk
Chester City Council	Environmental Planning, Backford Hall, Chester, CH1 6PZ; Tel: 01244 402245; www.chestercc.gov.uk
Chester-le-Street District Council	Planning Services (Development Group), Civic Centre, Newcastle Road, Chester le Street, DH3 3UT; Tel: 0191 3872146; www.chester-le-street.gov.uk
Chesterfield Borough Council	Directorate of Regeneration, Development Management (Planning Services), Town Hall, Rose Hill, Chesterfield, S40 1LP; Tel: 01246 345811; www.chesterfield.gov.uk
Chichester District Council	Development and Building Control Services, East Pallant House, 1 East Pallant, Chichester, PO19 1TY; Tel: 01243 785 166; www.chichester.gov.uk
Chiltern District Council	Planning and Environment, Council Offices, King George V Road, Amersham, HP6 5AW; Tel: 01494 732 042; www.chiltern.gov.uk
Chorley Borough Council	Planning Services, Civic Offices, Union Street, Chorley, Lancashire, PR7 IAL; Tel: 01257 515220; www.chorley.gov.uk
Christchurch Borough Council	Community Services Department, Civic Offices, Bridge Street, Christchurch, BH23 1AZ; Tel: 01202 495035; www.dorsetforyou.com

LIST OF PLANNING AUTHORITIES IN ENGLAND AND WALES

City of Lincoln Council	City Hall, Beaumont Fee, Lincoln, LN1 1DD; Tel: 01522 881188; www.lincoln.gov.uk
Colchester Borough Council	Lexden Grange, 127 Lexden Road, Colchester, CO3 3RJ; Tel: 01206 282424; www.colchester.gov.uk
Congleton Borough Council	Development & Building Control Section, Westfields, Middlewich Road, Sandbach, CW11 1HZ; Tel: 01270 763231; www.congleton.gov.uk
Copeland Borough Council	Development & Environment, PO Box 19, Council Offices, Catherine Street, Whitehaven, CA28 7NY; Tel: 01946 852585; www.copeland.gov.uk
Corby Borough Council	Deene House, New Post Office Square, Corby, NN17 1GD; Tel: 01536 464167; www.corby.gov.uk
Cotswold District Council	Planning Service, Trinity Road, Cirencester, GL7 1PX; Tel: 01285 623550; www.cotswold.gov.uk
Coventry City Council	Planning Control, Civic Centre, 4 Much Park Street, Coventry, CV1 2PY; Tel: 02476 831232; www.coventry.gov.uk
Craven District Council	Council Offices, Granville Street, Skipton, BD23 1PS; Tel: 01756 706470; www.cravendc.gov.uk
Crawley Borough Council	Environment and Housing Directorate, Town Hall, The Boulevard, Crawley, RH10 1UZ; Tel: 01293 438000; www.crawley.gov.uk
Crewe and Nantwich Borough Council	Development Control, Planning Division, Municipal Buildings, Earle Street, Crewe, CW1 2BJ; Tel: 01270 537490; www.crewe-nantwich.gov.uk
Dacorum Borough Council	Civic Centre, Marlowes, Hemel Hempstead, HP1 1HH; Tel: 01442 228376; www.dacorum.gov.uk
Darlington Borough Council	Development & Environment Department, Town Hall, Darlington, DL1 5QT; Tel: 01325 388670; www.darlington.gov.uk

LIST OF PLANNING AUTHORITIES IN ENGLAND AND WALES

Dartford Borough Council	Civic Centre, Home Gardens, Dartford, DA1 1DR; Tel: 01322 343203; www.dartford.gov.uk
Daventry District Council	Planning Control, Lodge Road, Daventry, NN11 5AF; Tel: 01327 302590; www.daventrydc.gov.uk
Derby City Council	Development & Cultural Services, Roman House, Friar Gate, Derby, DE1 1XB; Tel: 01332 255942; www.derby.gov.uk
Derbyshire Dales District Council	Environmental Services Department, North Block, County Hall, Matlock, DE4 3AG; Tel: 01629 580000; www.derbyshire.gov.uk
Derwentside District Council	Civic Centre, Medomsley Road, Consett, Co Durham, DH8 5JA; Tel: 01207 218276; www.derwentside.gov.uk/planning
Doncaster Metropolitan Borough Council	Directorate of Borough Strategy & Development Planning Services, 2nd Floor, Danum House, St Sepulchre Gate, Doncaster, DN1 1UB; Tel: 01302 734444; www.doncaster.gov.uk
Dover District Council	White Cliffs Business Park, Dover, Kent, CT16 3PJ; Tel: 01304 821199; www.dover.gov.uk
Dudley Metropolitan Borough Council	Directorate of the Urban Environment, 3 St James's Road, Dudley, DY1 1HZ; Tel: 01384 814116; www.dudley.gov.uk
Durham City Council	Environmental Services Department, Byland Lodge, Hawthorn Terrace, Durham, DH1 4TD; Tel: 0191 301 8700; www.durhamcity.gov.uk
Easington District Council	Planning & Building Control Services, Furze Hill, Seaside Lane, Easington, Peterlee, SR8 3TN; Tel: 0191 527 0501; www.easington.com
East Cambridgeshire District Council	Development Services, The Grange, Nutholt Lane, Ely, CB7 4PL; Tel: 01353 616225; www.eastcamb.gov.uk

LIST OF PLANNING AUTHORITIES IN ENGLAND AND WALES

East Devon District Council	Development Control Team Planning Department, Council Offices, Knowle, Sidmouth, EX10 8HL; Tel: 01395 516551; www.eastdevon.gov.uk
East Dorset District Council	Council Offices, Furzehill, Wimborne, BH21 4HN; Tel: 01202 886201; www.dorsetforyou.com
East Hampshire District Council	Planning Enquiries, Penns Place, Petersfield, GU31 4EX; Tel: 01730 234242; www.easthants.gov.uk
East Hertfordshire District Council	Development Control, Planning Department, Wallfields, Pegs Lane, Hertford, SG13 8EQ; Tel: 01279 655261; www.eastherts.gov.uk
East Lindsey District Council	Tedder Hall, Manby Park, Louth, LN11 8UP; Tel: 01507 601111; www.e-lindsey.gov.uk
East Northamptonshire Council	Development Control, Community Services Directorate, East Northamptonshire House, Cedar Drive, Thrapston, Kettering, NN14 4LZ; Tel: 01832 742000; www.east-northamptonshire.gov.uk
East Riding of Yorkshire Council	Planning & Development Control Department, AG19, County Hall Cross Street, Beverley, HU17 9BA; Tel: 0845 788 7700; www.eastriding.gov.uk
East Staffordshire Borough Council	Development Control, Midland Grain Warehouse, Derby Street, Burton-on-Trent, DE14 2JJ; Tel: 01283 508539; www.eaststaffbc.gov.uk
Eastbourne Borough Council	68 Grove Road, Eastbourne, BN21 4UH; Tel: 01323 415215; www.eastbourne.gov.uk
Eastleigh Borough Council	Development Control Services, Civic Offices, Leigh Road, Eastleigh, SO50 9YN; Tel: 023 8068 8248; www.eastleigh.gov.uk
Eden District Council	Planning Services, Mansion House, Friargate, Penrith, CA11 7YG; Tel: 01768 212363; www.eden.gov.uk

LIST OF PLANNING AUTHORITIES IN ENGLAND AND WALES

Harborough District Council	Planning, Council Offices, Adam & Eve Street, Market Harborough, LE16 7AG; Tel: 01858 821161; www.harborough.gov.uk
Harlow District Council	Planning Services, Development Control, 1 Adams House, The High, Harlow, CM20 1BD; Tel: 01279 446576; www.harlow.gov.uk
Harrogate Borough Council	Knapping Mount, West Grove Road, Harrogate, HG1 2AE; Tel: 01423 556666; www.harrogate.gov.uk
Hart District Council	Development Control Department, Civic Offices, Harlington Way, Fleet, GU51 4AE; Tel: 01252 622122; www.hart.gov.uk
Hartlepool Borough Council	Regeneration & Planning, Bryan Hanson House, Hanson Square, Hartlepool, TS24 7BT; Tel: 01429 523272; www.hartlepool.gov.uk
Hastings Borough Council	Regeneration & Planning, Century House, 100 Menzies Road, St Leonards on Sea, Hastings, TN38 9BB; Tel: 01424 783259; www.hastings.gov.uk
Havant Borough Council	Development Control, Civic Offices, Havant Civic Centre, Havant, PO9 2AX; Tel: 02392 446470; www.havant.gov.uk
Hertsemere Borough Council	Planning Unit, Civic Offices, Elstree Way, Borehamwood, WD6 1WA; Tel: 020 8207 2277; www.hertsmere.gov.uk
High Peak Borough Council	The Municipal Buildings, Glossop, SK13 8AF; Tel: 0845 129 77 77; www.highpeak.gov.uk
Hinckley & Bosworth Borough Council	Planning Department, Council Offices, Argents Mead, Hinckley, Leicester, LE10 1BZ; Tel: 01455 238141; www.hinckley-bosworth.gov.uk
Horsham District Council	Development Control, North & South Team, Park House, North Street, Horsham, RH12 1RL; Tel: 01403 215191; www.horsham.gov.uk

LIST OF PLANNING AUTHORITIES IN ENGLAND AND WALES

Huntingdonshire District Council	Planning Division, Pathfinder House, St Marys Street, Huntingdon, PE29 3TN; Tel: 01480 388388; www.huntsdc.gov.uk
Hyndburn Borough Council	Planning & Transportation Department, Scaitcliffe House, Omerod Street, Accrington, BB5 0PF; Tel: 01254 388111; www.hyndburnbc.gov.uk
Ipswich Borough Council	The Civic Centre, Civic Drive, Ipswich, IP1 2EE; Tel: 01473 432912; www.ipswich.gov.uk
Isle of Wight Council	Development Control, Seaclose Offices, Fairlee Road, Newport, PO30 2QS; Tel: 01983 823552; www.iwight.com
Kennet District Council	Community Services Department, Browfort, Bath Road, Devizes, SN10 2AT; Tel: 01380 721185; www.kennet.gov.uk
Kerrier District Council	Planning Service, Dolcoath Avenue, Camborne, TR14 8SX; Tel: 01209 614000; www.kerrier.gov.uk
Kettering Borough Council	Development Services, Municipal Offices, Bowling Green Road, Kettering, NN15 7QX; Tel: 01536 410333; www.kettering.gov.uk
Kingston-upon-Hull City Council	Planning, Kingston House, Bond Street, Kingston-upon-Hull, HU1 3ER; Tel: 01482 300 300; www.hullcc.gov.uk
King's Lynn & West Norfolk Borough Council	Planning Control, Kings' Court, Chapel Street, King's Lynn, PE30 1EX; Tel: 01553 616200; www.west-norfolk.gov.uk
Kirklees Metropolitan Borough Council	Planning Services, Development Control, Civic Centre III, PO Box B93, Huddersfield, HD1 2JR; Tel: 01484 221504; www.kirklees.gov.uk
Knowsley Metropolitan Borough Council	Regeneration & Development, PO Box 26, Municipal Buildings, Archway Road, Huyton, L36 9FB; Tel: 0151 443 2316; www.knowsley.gov.uk
Lancaster City Council	Development Control, Palatine Hall, Dalton Square, Lancaster, LA1 1PW; Tel: 01524 582338; www.lancaster.gov.uk

LIST OF PLANNING AUTHORITIES IN ENGLAND AND WALES

Leeds City Council	Planning Services, Development Department, The Leonardo Building, 2 Rossington Street, Leeds, LS2 8HD; Tel: 0113 247 8000; www.leeds.gov.uk
Leicester City Council	Development Control Group, 8th Floor, A Block, New Walk Centre, Welford Place, Leicester, LE1 6ZG; Tel: 0116 254 9922; www.leicester.gov.uk
Lewes District Council	Environment & Planning, PO Box 168, Lewes, East Sussex, BN7 9FA; Tel: 01273 471600; www.lewes.gov.uk
Lichfield District Council	District Council House, Frog Lane, Lichfield, WS13 6YZ; Tel: 01543 308152; www.lichfielddc.gov.uk
Liverpool City Council	Planning & Building Control, 2nd Floor, Millennium House, 60 Victoria Street, Liverpool, L1 6JF; Tel: 0151 233 3021; www.liverpool.gov.uk
Luton Borough Council	Department of Environment & Regeneration, Town Hall, Luton, LU1 2BQ; Tel: 01582 546305; www.luton.gov.uk
Macclesfield Borough Council	Planning Department, Town Hall, Market Square, Macclesfield, SK10 1DP; Tel: 01625 504649; www.macclesfield.gov.uk
Maidstone Borough Council	Regulatory Services, 13 Tonbridge Road, Maidstone, ME16 8HG; Tel: 01622 602000; www.digitalmaidstone.co.uk
Maldon District Council	Planning Department, Council Offices, Princes Road, Maldon, CM9 5DL; Tel: 01621 875737; www.maldon.gov.uk
Malvern Hills District Council	Planning Services Department, Brunel House, Portland Road, Malvern, WR14 2TB; Tel: 01684 892700; www.malvernhills.gov.uk
Manchester City Council	Regeneration Division (planning), Town Hall Extension, PO Box 463, Manchester, M60 3NY; Tel: 0161 234 4071; www.manchester.gov.uk

LIST OF PLANNING AUTHORITIES IN ENGLAND AND WALES

Mansfield District Council	Planning & Building Control, Civic Centre, Chesterfield Road South, Mansfield, NG19 7BH; Tel: 01623 463069; www.mansfield.gov.uk
Medway Council	Planning & Transport Directorate, Compass Centre, Chatham Maritime, Chatham Maritime, ME7 4YH; Tel: 01634 331700; www.medway.gov.uk
Melton Borough Council	Development Control, Council Offices, Nottingham Road, Melton Mowbray, LE13 0UL; Tel: 01664 502503; www.meltononline.co.uk
Mendip District Council	Planning & Environment Department, Council Offices, Cannards Grave Road, Shepton Mallet, BA4 5BT; Tel: 01749 341550; www.mendip.gov.uk
Middlesbrough Borough Council	Planning & Development Services, PO Box 65, Vancouver House, Gurney Street, Middlesbrough, TS1 1QP; Tel: 01642 728060; www.middlesbrough.gov.uk
Mid Bedfordshire District Council	Planning Department, 23 London Road, Biggleswade, SG18 8ER; Tel: 01767 602357; www.midbeds.gov.uk
Mid Devon District Council	Ailsa House, Tidcombe Lane, Tiverton, EX16 4DZ; Tel: 01884 234274; www.middevon.gov.uk
Mid Suffolk District Council	Planning Control Section, Council Offices, 131 High Street, Needham Market, Ipswich, IP6 8DL; Tel: 01449 727452; www.midsuffolk.gov.uk
Mid Sussex District Council	Environment Directorate, Oaklands Road, Haywards Heath, RH16 1SS; Tel: 01444 477462; www.midsussex.gov.uk
Milton Keynes Borough Council	Planning Department, Civic Offices, 1 Saxon Gate East, Milton Keynes MK9 3HQ; Tel: 01908 252599; www.milton-keynes.gov.uk
Mole Valley District Council	Planning Department, Council Offices, Council Offices, Pippbrook, Dorking, RH4 1SJ; Tel: 01306 879237; www.mole-valley.gov.uk

LIST OF PLANNING AUTHORITIES IN ENGLAND AND WALES

Newark & Sherwood District Council	Planning Services, Kelham Hall, Newark, Notts, NG23 5QX; Tel: 01636 655888; www.newark-sherwooddc.gov.uk
Newcastle-under-Lyme Borough Council	Planning Services Department, Civic Offices, Merrial Street, Newcastle-under-Lyme, ST5 2AG; Tel: 01782 742441; www.newcastle-staffs.gov.uk
Newcastle upon Tyne City Council	Legal Services, Civic Centre, Barras Bridge, Newcastle upon Tyne, NE99 2BN; Tel: 0191 211 5117; www.newcastle.gov.uk
New Forest District Council	Directorate of Environment Services, Development Control Section, Appletree Court, Lyndhurst, SO43 7PA; Tel: 02380 285000; www.newforest.gov.uk
Northampton Borough Council	Development Control, Planning Services, Cliftonville House, Bedford Road, Northampton, NN4 7NR; Tel: 01604 838910; www.northampton.gov.uk
North Cornwall District Council	Planning & Development Department, 3–5 Barn Lane, Bodmin, PL31 1LZ; Tel: 01208 893333; www.ncdc.gov.uk
North Devon District Council	Planning, Civic Centre, Barnstaple, Devon, EX31 1EA; Tel: 01271 327711; www.northdevon.gov.uk
North Dorset District Council	Development Control, Nordon, Salisbury Road, Blandford Forum, DT11 7LL; Tel: 01258 454111; www.north-dorset.gov.uk
North East Derbyshire District Council	Planning & Development Department, Council House, Saltergate, Chesterfield, S40 1LF; Tel: 01246 212648; www.ne-derbyshire.gov.uk
North East Lincolnshire Council	Development & Environmental Protection; Civic Offices, Knoll Street, Cleethorpes, DN35 8LN; Tel: 01472 324259; www.nelincs.gov.uk

LIST OF PLANNING AUTHORITIES IN ENGLAND AND WALES

North Hertfordshire District Council	Development Control, Environment Services Department, Council Offices, Gernon Road, Garden City, Letchworth, SG6 3JF; Tel: 01462 474206; www.north-herts.gov.uk
North Kesteven District Council	Planning Services, District Council Offices, 3 Kesteven Street, Sleaford, NG34 7EF; Tel: 01529 414155; www.n-kesteven.gov.uk
North Lincolnshire District Council	Development Control Team, Council Offices, PO Box 42, Church Square House, Scunthorpe, DN15 6XQ; Tel: 01724 297420; www.northlincs.gov.uk
North Norfolk District Council	Planning Service, Council Offices, Holt Road, Cromer, Norfolk, NR27 9EN; Tel: 01263 513811; www.northnorfolk.org
North Shropshire District Council	Planning Services Department, Development Control, Edinburgh House, New Street, Wem, SY4 5DB; Tel: 01939 232771; www.northshropshire.gov.uk
North Somerset Council	Development Control Group, Somerset House, Oxford Street, Weston-super-Mare, BS23 1TG; Tel: 01275 888663; www.n-somerset.gov.uk
North Tyneside Council	The Killingworth Site, PO Box 113, Station Road, Killingworth, Newcastle upon Tyne, NE12 6WJ; Tel: 0191 219 2195; www.northtyneside.gov.uk
North Warwickshire Borough Council	Department of Planning & Economic Strategy, PO Box 43, Shire Hall, Warwick, CV34 4SX; Tel: 01926 412906; www.warwickshire.gov.uk
North West Leicestershire District Council	Planning Department; Council Offices, Whitwick Road, Coalville, Leicester, LE67 3FJ; Tel: 01530 454668; www.nwleicsdc.gov.uk

LIST OF PLANNING AUTHORITIES IN ENGLAND AND WALES

North Wiltshire District Council	Development Control Section, Monkton Park, Chippenham, SN15 1ER; Tel: 01249 706654; www.northwilts.gov.uk
Norwich City Council	Development Directorate, City Hall, St Peters Street, Norwich, NR2 1WP; Tel: 01603 212500; www.norwich.gov.uk
Nottingham City Council	Planning Applications & Advice, 3rd Floor, Exchange Buildings North, Smithy Row, Nottingham, NG1 2BS; Tel: 0115 915 5426; www.plan4nottingham.co.uk
Nuneaton and Bedworth Borough Council	Development Control Section, Town Hall, Coton Road, Nuneaton, CV11 5AA; Tel: 02476 378328; www.nuneatonandbedworth.gov.uk
Oadby & Wigston Borough Council	Development Control Section, Council Offices, Station Road, Wigston, Leicester, LE18 2DR; Tel: 0116 257 2655; www.oadby-wigston.gov.uk
Oldham Metropolitan Borough	Environmental Services Department, PO Box 30, Civic Centre, West Street, Oldham, OL1 1UQ; Tel: 0161 911 4105; www.oldham.gov.uk
Oswestry Borough Council	Planning Services, Development Services Section, Castle View, Oswestry, SY11 1JR; Tel: 01691 671111; www.oswestry.gov.uk
Oxford City Council	Planning, Ramsay House, 10 St Ebbe's Street, Oxford, OX1 1PT; Tel: 01865 252143; www.oadby-wigston.gov.uk
Pendle Borough Council	Planning & Building Control, Town Hall, Market Street, Nelson, BB9 7LG; Tel: 01282 661708; www.pendle.gov.uk
Penwith District Council	Planning & Building Control, Council Offices, St Clare, Penzance, TR18 3QW; Tel: 01736 336788; www.penwith.gov.uk
Peterborough City Council	Development Control & Enforcement Section, Bridge House, Town Bridge, Peterborough, PE11HB; Tel: 01733 453410; www.peterborough.gov.uk

LIST OF PLANNING AUTHORITIES IN ENGLAND AND WALES

Plymouth City Council	Department of Development, Civic Centre, Floor 8, Plymouth, PL1 2EW; Tel: 01752 668000; www.plymouth.gov.uk
Poole Borough Council	Planning & Development Services, Civic Centre, Poole, BH15 2RU; Tel: 01202 633633; www.poole.gov.uk
Portsmouth City Council	Planning Services, Civic Offices, Portsmouth, PO1 2AU; Tel: 023 9283 4334; www.portsmouth.gov.uk
Preston Borough Council	Environmental Services, Lancastria House, 77–79 Lancaster Road, Preston, PR1 2RH; Tel: 01772 906581; www.preston.gov.uk
Purbeck District Council	Development & Building Control Section, Westport House, Worgret Road, Wareham, BH20 4PP; Tel: 01929 556561; www.purbeck.gov.uk
Reading Borough Council	Environment Directorate, Civic Centre, Reading, RG1 7TD; Tel: 0118 626540; www.reading.gov.uk
Redcar and Cleveland Council	Redcar and Cleveland House, Kirkleatham Street, Redcar, TS10 1YA; Tel: 01287 612344; www.redcar-cleveland.gov.uk
Redditch Borough Council	Development Control Department, Town Hall, Alcester Street, Redditch, B98 8AH; Tel: 01527 64252; www.redditchbc.gov.uk
Reigate and Banstead Borough Council	Building & Development Services, Town Hall, Castlefield Road, Reigate, RH2 0SH; Tel: 01737 276000; www.reigate-banstead.gov.uk
Restormel Borough Council	Planning Department, Borough Offices, 39 Penwinnick Road, St Austell, PL25 5DR; Tel: 01726 223300; www.restormel.gov.uk

LIST OF PLANNING AUTHORITIES IN ENGLAND AND WALES

Ribble Valley Borough Council	Development Department, Council Offices, Church Walk, Clitheroe, BB7 2RA; Tel: 01200 425111; www.ribblevalley.gov.uk
Richmondshire District Council	Swale House, Frenchgate, Richmond, North Yorkshire, DL10 4JE; Tel: 01748 829100; www.richmondshire.gov.uk
Rochdale Metropolitan Borough Council	Planning & Regulation Services, PO Box 32, Telegraph House, Baillie Street, Rochdale, OL16 1JH; Tel: 01706 864308; www.rochdale.gov.uk
Rochford District Council	Planning Services, Council Offices, South Street, Rochford, SS4 1BW; Tel: 01702 546366; www.rochford.gov.uk
Rossendale Borough Council	Development Control Section, Stubbylee Hall, Bacup, OL13 0DE; Tel: 01706 217777; www.rossendale.gov.uk
Rother District Council	Town Hall, Bexhill on Sea, TN39 3JX; Tel: 01424 787600; www.planning.rother.gov.uk
Rotherham Metropolitan Borough Council	The Town Hall, The Crofts, Moorgate Street, Rotherham, South Yorkshire, S60 2TH; Tel: 01709 822740; www.rotherham.gov.uk
Rugby Borough Council	Planning Department, PO Box 123, Town Hall, Rugby, CV21 2ZP; Tel: 01788 533533; www.rugby.gov.uk
Runnymede Borough Council	Planning Division, Civic Offices, Station Road, Addlestone, Weybridge, KT15 2AH; Tel: 01932 838383; www.runnymede.gov.uk
Rushcliffe Borough Council	Borough Development, Civic Centre, Pavilion Road, West Bridgford, Nottingham, NG2 5FE; Tel: 0115 981 9911; www.rushcliffe.gov.uk
Rushmoor Borough Council	Planning Services, Council Offices, Farnborough Road, Farnborough, GU14 7JU; Tel: 01252 398398; www.rushmoor.gov.uk
Ryedale District Council	Development Control, Ryedale House, Malton, YO17 7HH; Tel: 01653 600666; www.ryedale.gov.uk

LIST OF PLANNING AUTHORITIES IN ENGLAND AND WALES

St Albans District Council	Development Control, District Council Offices, Civic Centre, St Peters Street, St Albans, AL1 3JE; Tel: 01727 866100; www.stalbans.gov.uk
St Edmundsbury Borough Council	St Edmundsbury House, PO Box 122, Western Way, Bury St Edmunds, IP33 3YS; Tel: 01284 763 233; www.stedmundsbury.gov.uk
St Helens Metropolitan Borough Council	Town Planning, 1st Floor, Town Hall, Victoria Square, St Helens, WA10 1HP; Tel: 01744 456119; www.sthelens.gov.uk
Salford Metropolitan Borough Council	Building & Development Control Services, Civic Centre, Chorley Road, Swinton, Manchester, M27 5BW; Tel: 0161 793 3654; www.salford.gov.uk
Salisbury District Council	Planning Office, 61 Wyndham Road, Salisbury, SP1 3AH; Tel: 01722 434375; www.salisbury.gov.uk
Sandwell Metropolitan Borough Council	Development House, PO Box 42, Lombard Street, West Bromwich, B70 8RU; Tel: 0121 569 4032; www.sandwell.gov.uk
Scarborough Borough Council	Department of Technical Services, Town Hall, St Nicholas Street, Scarborough, YO11 2HG; Tel: 01723 232477; www.e-sbc.co.uk
Sedgefield Borough Council	Planning & Technical Services, Development Control, Council Offices, Spennymoor, DL16 6JQ; Tel: 01388 816166; www.sedgefield.gov.uk
Sedgemoor District Council	Development Services, Bridgwater House, Kings Square, Bridgwater, TA6 3AR; Tel: 01278 435246; www.sedgemoor.gov.uk
Sefton Metropolitan Borough Council	Planning Department, Magdalen House, 30 Trinity Road, Bootle, L20 3NJ; Tel: 0151 934 3580; www.sefton.gov.uk
Selby District Council	Development Control, Civic Centre, Portholme Road, Selby, YO8 4SB; Tel: 01757 292010; www.selby.gov.uk

LIST OF PLANNING AUTHORITIES IN ENGLAND AND WALES

Sevenoaks District Council	Development Control, PO Box 183, Council Offices, Argyle Road, Sevenoaks, TN13 1HG; Tel: 01732 227000; www.sevenoaks.gov.uk
Sheffield City Council	Development Control, Development Services, Howden House, 1 Union Street, Sheffield, S1 2SH; Tel: 0114 223 5499; www.sheffield.gov.uk
Shepway District Council	Planning Control Department, Room 110, Civic Centre, Castle Hill Avenue, Folkestone, CT20 2QY; Tel: 01303 850 388; www.shepway.gov.uk
Shrewsbury & Atcham Borough Council	The Guildhall, Frankwell Quay, Shrewsbury, SY3 8HQ; Tel: 01743 281000; www.shrewsbury.gov.uk
Slough Borough Council	Landmark Place, High Street, Slough, SL1 1OL; Tel: 01753 475111; www.slough.gov.uk
Solihull Metropolitan Borough Council	Development Control & Conservation, PO Box 18, Council House, Solihull, B91 9QS; Tel: 0121 704 6000; www.solihull.gov.uk
South Bedfordshire District Council	High Street North, Dunstable, LU6 1LF; Tel: 01582 472222; www.southbeds.gov.uk
South Bucks District Council	Development Control, Council Offices, Windsor Road, Slough, SL1 2HN; Tel: 01753 533333 (or Capswood, Oxford Road, Denham, Bucks, UB9 4LH; Tel: 01895 837 200); www.southbucks.gov.uk
South Cambridgeshire District Council	South Cambridgeshire Hall, Cambourne Business Park, Cambourne, Cambridge, CB23 6EA; Tel: 08450 450 500; www.scambs.gov.uk
South Derbyshire District Council	Civic Office, Civic Way, Swandlincote, DE11 OAH; Tel: 01283 595795; www.south-derbys.gov.uk
South Gloucestershire District Council	Planning, Transportation & Strategic Environment, Council Offices, Castle Street, Thornbury, BS35 1HF; Tel: 01454 868686; www.southglos.gov.uk

LIST OF PLANNING AUTHORITIES IN ENGLAND AND WALES

South Hams District Council	Follaton House, Plymouth Road, Totnes, TO9 5NE; Tel: 01803 861277; www.southhams.gov.uk
South Holland District Council	Planning & Development Services, 1st Floor, Council Offices, Priory Road, Spalding, PE11 2XE; Tel: 01775 761161; www.sholland.gov.uk
South Kesteven District Council	Land Use Planning Services, Council Offices, St Peters Hill, Grantham, NG31 6PZ; Tel: 01476 406080; www.skdc.com
South Lakeland District Council	Planning Services, South Lakeland House, Lowther Street, Kendal, LA9 4UG; Tel: 01539 733333; www.southlakeland.gov.uk
South Norfolk District Council	Planning & Development Control Services, South Norfolk House, Swan Lane, Long Stratton, Norwich, NR15 2XE; Tel: 01508 533633; www.south-norfolk.gov.uk
South Oxfordshire District Council	Benson Lane, Crowmarsh Gifford, Wallingford, OX10 8ED; Tel: 01491 823000; www.southoxon.gov.uk
South Northamptonshire Council	Planning & Leisure Division, Springfields, Towcester, NN12 6AE; Tel: 01327 322322; www.southnorthants.gov.uk
South Ribble Borough Council	Planning & Regeneration Department, Civic Centre, West Paddock, Leyland, PR25 1DH; Tel: 01772 421491; www.southribble.gov.uk
South Shropshire District Council	Environment & Development, Planning & Building Control, Stone House, Corve Street, Ludlow, SY8 1DG; Tel: 01584 813360; www.southshropshire.gov.uk
South Somerset District Council	Council Offices, Brympton Way, Yeovil, Somerset, BA20 2HT; Tel: 01935 462462; www.southsomerset.gov.uk
South Staffordshire District Council	Development & Building Control, Council Offices, Wolverhampton Road, Codsall, Nr Wolverhampton, WV8 1PX; Tel: 01902 696000; www.sstaffs.gov.uk

LIST OF PLANNING AUTHORITIES IN ENGLAND AND WALES

South Tyneside Metropolitan Borough Council	Town Hall & Civic Offices, Westoe Road, South Shields, NE33 2RL; Tel: 0191 427 1717; www.southtyneside.info
Southampton City Council	Planning & Sustain Ability Division, Development Control Services, Civic Centre, Southampton, SO14 7LY; Tel: 023 8022 3855; www.southampton.gov.uk
Southend Borough Council	Technical & Environmental Services Department, 10th Floor, Civic Centre, Victoria Avenue, Southend on Sea, SS2 6ER; Tel: 01702 215000; www.southend.gov.uk
Spelthorne Borough Council	Development Control Section, Council Offices, Knowle Green, Staines, TW18 1XB; Tel: 01784 451 499; www.spelthorne.gov.uk
Stafford Borough Council	Civic Centre, Riverside, Stafford, ST16 3AQ; Tel: 01785 619302; www.staffordbc.gov.uk
Staffordshire Moorlands District Council	Development Control, Moorlands House, Stockwell Street, Leek, ST13 6HQ; Tel: 0845 605 3013; www.staffmoorlands.gov.uk
Stevenage Borough Council	Development Control, Daneshill House, Danestrete, Stevenage, SG1 1HN; Tel: 01438 242242; www.stevenage.gov.uk
Stockport Metropolitan Borough Council	Hygarth House, 103 Wellington Road South, Stockport, SK1 3TT; Tel: 0161 474 3617; www.stockport.gov.uk/planning
Stockton-on-Tees Borough Council	Development Control, Planning & Environment, Ground Floor, Muncipal Buildings, Church Road, TS18 1LD; Tel: 01642 393939; www.stockton-bc.gov.uk
Stoke-on-Trent City Council	Directorate of Urban Environment, PO Box 630, Civic Centre, Glebe Street, Stoke on Trent, ST4 1RF; Tel: 01782 232435; www.stoke.gov.uk

LIST OF PLANNING AUTHORITIES IN ENGLAND AND WALES

Stratford on Avon District Council	Regulatory Services, Elizabeth House, Church Street, Stratford Upon Avon, CV37 6HX; Tel: 01789 267575; www.stratford.gov.uk
Stroud District Council	Development Services, Ebley Mill, Westward Road, Stroud, GL5 4UB; Tel: 01453 766321; www.stroud.gov.uk
Suffolk Coastal District Council	Development & Community Services, Development Control Teams, Council Offices, Melton Hill, Woodbridge, IP12 1AU; Tel: 01394 383789; www.suffolkcoastal.gov.uk
Sunderland City Council	Development & Regeneration, Civic Centre, PO Box 102, Burdon Road, Sunderland, SR2 7DN; Tel: 0191 553 1000; www.sunderland.gov.uk
Surrey Heath Borough Council	Planning & Community Services, Surreyheath House, Knoll Road, Camberley, GU15 3HD; Tel: 01276 707100; www.surreyheath.gov.uk
Swale Borough Council	Planning & Economic Development, Swale House, East Street, Sittingbourne, Kent, ME10 3HT; Tel: 01795 417850; www.swale.gov.uk
Swindon Borough Council	Civic Offices, Euclid Street, Swindon, SN1 2JH; Tel: 01793 445500; www.swindon.gov.uk
Tameside Metropolitan Borough Council	Planning & Building Control, Council Offices, Wellington Road, Ashton under Lyme, OL6 6DL; Tel: 0161 342 8355; www.tameside.gov.uk
Tamworth Borough Council	Planning & Regeneration Department, Municpal Offices, Marmion House, Lichfield Street, Tamworth, B79 7BZ; Tel: 01827 709709; www.tamworth.gov.uk
Tandridge District Council	Council Offices, Station Road East, Oxted, RH8 0BT; Tel: 01883 722 000; www.tandridge.gov.uk
Taunton Deane Borough Council	The Deane House, Belvedere Road, Taunton, TA1 1HE; Tel: 01823 356356; www.tauntondeane.gov.uk

LIST OF PLANNING AUTHORITIES IN ENGLAND AND WALES

Teesdale District Council	Planning Department, Development Control, Teesdale House, Galgate, Barnard Castle, County Durham, DL12 8EL; Tel: 01833 690000; www.teesdale.gov.uk
Teignbridge District Council	Planning Department, Forde House, Brunel Road, Newton Abbot, TQ12 4XX; Tel: 01626 361101; www.teignbridge.gov.uk
Telford & Wrekin Council	Development & Design, Darby House, PO Box 212, Telford, TF3 4LB; Tel: 01952 380 000; www.telford.gov.uk
Tendring District Council	Regeneration, Planning & Community Services, Council Offices, Thorpe Road, Weeley, Clacton on Sea, CO16 9AJ; Tel: 01255 686868; www.tendringdc.gov.uk
Test Valley Borough Council	Planning Department, Council Offices, Beech Hurst, Weyhill Road, Andover, SP10 3AJ; Tel: 01264 368000 (or Planning Support Team, Council Offices, Duttons Road, Romsey, SO51 8XG; Tel: 01794 527700); www.testvalley.gov.uk
Tewkesbury Borough Council	Planning Department, Council Offices, Gloucester Road, Tewkesbury, GL20 5TT; Tel: 01684 272111; www.tewkesburybc.com
Thanet District Council	Planning Services, Council Offices, PO Box 9, Cecil Street, Margate, CT9 1XZ; Tel: 01843 577000; www.thanet.gov.uk
Three Rivers District Council	Community & Environmental Services, Three Rivers House, Northway, Rickmansworth, Herts, WD3 1RL; Tel: 01923 776611; www.threerivers.gov.uk
Thurrock Council	Environmental Services Department, Floor 2, Civic Offices, New Road, Grays, RM17 6SL; Tel: 01375 652652; www.thurrock.gov.uk
Torbay Borough Council	Planning Services, Roebuck House, Abbey Road, Torquay, TQ2 5DP; Tel: 01803 207 801; www.torbay.gov.uk

LIST OF PLANNING AUTHORITIES IN ENGLAND AND WALES

Tonbridge & West Malling Borough Council	Development Control, Gibson Building, Gibson Drive, Kings Hill, West Malling, ME19 4LZ; Tel: 01732 844522; www.tmbc.gov.uk
Torridge District Council	Planning & Technical Services Department, Riverbank House, Bideford, EX39 2QG; Tel: 01237 428700; www.torridge.gov.uk
Trafford Metropolitan Borough Council	Planning & Building Control, PO Box 12, Trafford Town Hall, Talbot Road, Stretford, M32 0YT; Tel: 0161 912 2000; www.trafford.gov.uk
Tunbridge Wells Borough Council	Planning & Building Control Section, Town Hall, Royal Tunbridge Wells, Kent, TN1 1RS; Tel: 01892 526 121; www.tunbridgewells.gov.uk
Tynedale District Council	Planning Department, Old Grammar School, Hallgate, Hexham, NE46 1XA; Tel: 01434 652121; www.tynedale.gov.uk
Uttlesford District Council	Development Control, Council Offices, London Road, Saffron Walden, CB11 4ER; Tel: 01799 510467; www.uttlesford.gov.uk
Vale Royal Borough Council	Development Services, Wyvern House, The Drumber, Winsford, CW7 1AH; Tel: 01606 862862; www.valeroyal.gov.uk
Vale of White Horse District Council	PO Box 127, Abbey House, Abbey Close, Abingdon, OX14 3JE; Tel: 01235 520202; www.whitehorsedc.gov.uk
Wakefield Metropolitan District Council	Newton Bar, Leeds Road, Wakefield, WF1 2TX; Tel: 01924 306595; www.wakefield.gov.uk
Walsall Metropolitan Borough Council	Planning Services, Civic Centre, Walsall, WS1 1TP; Tel: 01922 650 000; www.walsall.gov.uk
Wansbeck District Council	Borough Planners Service, The Town Hall, Wandsworth High Street, SW18 2PU; Tel: 020 8871 8871; www.wandsworth.gov.uk

LIST OF PLANNING AUTHORITIES IN ENGLAND AND WALES

Warrington Borough Council	26—30 Horsemarket Street, Warrington, Cheshire, WA1 1XL; Tel: 01925 443211; www.warrington.gov.uk
Warwick District Council	Planning & Engineering Department, PO Box 2178, Riverside House, Milverton Hill, Leamington Spa, CV32 5QH; Tel: 01926 456538; www.warwickdc.gov.uk
Watford Borough Council	Planning, Town Hall, Watford, Hertfordshire, WD17 3EX; Tel: 01923 226400; www.watford.gov.uk
Waveney District Council	Town Hall, High Street, Lowestoft, Suffolk, NR32 1HS; Tel: 01502 562111; www.waveney.gov.uk
Waverley Borough Council	Planning & Development Department, Council Offices, The Burys, Godalming, GU7 1HR; Tel: 01483 523583; www.waverley.gov.uk
Wealden District Council	Council Offices, Pine Grove, Crowborough, TN6 1DH; Tel: 01892 653311; www.wealden.gov.uk
Wear Valley District Council	Civic Centre, Crook, DL15 9ES; Tel: 01388 765555; www.wearvalley.gov.uk
Wellingborough Borough Council	Swanspool House, Doddington Road, Wellingborough, NN8 1BP; Tel: 01933 229777; www.wellingborough.gov.uk
Welwyn Hatfield District Council	Council Offices, The Campus, Welwyn Garden City, AL8 6AE; Tel: 01707 357 000; www.welhat.gov.uk
West Berkshire Council	Planning & Trading Standards, Council Offices, Market Street, Newbury, Berkshire, RG14 5LD; Tel: 01635 42400; www.westberks.gov.uk
West Devon Borough Council	Planning & Building Control, Kilworthy Park, Drake Road, Tavistock, PL19 0BZ; Tel: 01822 813600; www.westdevon.gov.uk
West Dorset District Council	Development Control Division, Stratton House, 58-60 High West Street, Dorchester, DT1 1UZ; Tel: 01305 251010; www.dorsetforyou.com

LIST OF PLANNING AUTHORITIES IN ENGLAND AND WALES

West Lancashire District Council	Development Control, 52 Derby Street, Ormskirk, L39 2DF; Tel: 01695 577177; www.westlancsdc.gov.uk
West Lindsey District Council	Development Control Section, 26 Spital Terrace, Gainsborough, DN21 2HG; Tel: 01427 676676; www.west-lindsey.gov.uk
West Oxfordshire District Council	Area Planning Manager, Council Offices, Elmfield, New Yatt Road, Witney, OX28 1BV; Tel: 01993 861000; www.westoxon.gov.uk
West Somerset District Council	West Somerset House, Killick Way, Williton, Taunton, TA4 4QA; Tel: 01643 703 704; www.westsomerset.gov.uk
West Wiltshire District Council	Development Control Department, Council Offices, Bradley Road, Trowbridge, BA14 0RD; Tel: 01225 776 655; www.westwiltshire.gov.uk
Weymouth and Portland Borough Council	Environmental Services, Development Control Planning, Council Offices, North Quay, Weymouth, DT4 8TA; Tel: 01305 838000; www.weymouth.gov.uk
Wigan Metropolitan Borough Council	Planning & Development Department, Civic Buildings, New Market Street, Wigan, WN1 1RP; Tel: 01942 244991; www.wiganmbc.gov.uk
Winchester City Council	Colebrook Street, Winchester, Hampshire, SO23 9LJ; Tel: 01962 840 222; www.winchester.gov.uk
Windsor & Maidenhead, Royal Borough of	Town Hall, St Ives Road, Maidenhead, Berkshire, SL6 1RF; Tel: 01628 683 810; www.rbwm.gov.uk
Wirral Metropolitan Borough Council	Planning & Economic Development Department, Town Hall, Brighton Street, Wallasey, Wirral, CH44 8ED; Tel: 0151 606 2000; www.wirral.gov.uk
Woking Borough Council	Civic Offices, Gloucester Square, Woking, Surrey, GU21 6YL; Tel: 01483 755855; www.woking.gov.uk

LIST OF PLANNING AUTHORITIES IN ENGLAND AND WALES

Wokingham District Council	Planning Services, PO Box 157, Shute End, Wokingham, RG11 1BN; Tel: 0118 974 6000; www.wokingham.gov.uk
Wolverhampton City Council	Regeneration & Transportation Planning Services, Civic Centre, St Peters Square, Wolverhampton, WV1 1RP; Tel: 01902 551155; www.wolverhampton.gov.uk
Worcester City Council	Development Services, Orchard House, Farrier Street, Worcester, WR1 3BB; Tel: 01905 722532; www.cityofworcester.gov.uk
Worthing Borough Council	Portland House, Richmond Road, Worthing, BN11 1LF; Tel: 01903 239999; www.worthing.gov.uk
Wychavon District Council	Planning Services, Civic Centre, Queen Elizabeth Drive, Pershore, WR10 1PT; Tel: 01386 565000; www.wychavon.gov.uk
Wycombe District Council	Planning & Major Projects, Development Control, Queen Victoria Road, High Wycombe, HP11 1BB; Tel: 01494 421539; www.wycombe.gov.uk
Wyre Borough Council	Planning Division, Civic Centre, Breck Road, Poulton Le Fylde, FY6 7PU; Tel: 01253 891 000; www.wyrebc.gov.uk/planning.htm
Wyre Forest District Council	Planning, Health & Environment, Duke House, Clensmore Street, Kidderminster, Worcestershire, DY10 2JX; Tel: 01562 732928; www.wyreforestdc.gov.uk
York City Council	Plans Processing Unit, 9 St Leonard's Place, York, YO1 7ET; Tel: 01904 551 553; www.york.gov.uk
GREATER LONDON	
Barking & Dagenham Borough Council	Development Control Team Town Hall, 1 Town Square, Barking, 1G11 7LU; Tel: 020 8215 3000; www.barking-dagenham.gov.uk

LIST OF PLANNING AUTHORITIES IN ENGLAND AND WALES

Barnet Borough Council	North London Business Park (NLBP), Oakleigh Road South, London, N11 1NP; Tel: 020 8359 2000; www.barnet.gov.uk
Bexley Borough Council	Bexley Civic Offices, Broadway, Bexleyheath, Kent, DA6 7LB; Tel: 020 8303 77777; www.bexley.gov.uk
Brent Borough Council	The Planning Service, Brent House, 349–357 High Road, Wembley, HA9 6BZ; Tel: 020 8937 1200; www.brent.gov.uk
Bromley Borough Council	Town Planning, Civic Centre, Stockwell Close, Bromley, BR1 3UH; Tel: 020 8464 3333; www.bromley.gov.uk
Camden Borough Council	Development Control Planning Services, 5th Floor, Town Hall Extension, Argyle Street, London, WC1H 8EQ; Tel: 020 7974 5613; www.camden.gov.uk
Corporation of London	Planning & Transportation Department, City Planning Officer, Peter Rees, PO Box 270, Guildhall, London, EC2P 2EJ; Tel: 020 7332 1710; www.cityoflondon.gov.uk/Corporation
Croydon Borough Council	Planning and Development Department, Taberner House, Park Lane, Croydon, CR9 1JT; Tel: 020 8726 6800; www.croydon.gov.uk/planning
Ealing Borough Council	Planning Services, 1st Floor, Perceval House, 14–16 Uxbridge Road, London, W5 2HL; Tel: 020 8825 6600; www.ealing.gov.uk
Enfield Borough Council	Planning & Transportation, Development Control, PO Box 53, Silver Street, Enfield, EN1 3XE; Tel: 020 8379 1000; www.enfield.gov.uk
Greenwich Borough Council	London Borough of Greenwich, Town Hall, Wellington Street, Woolwich, London, SE18 6PW; Tel: 020 8854 8888; www.greenwich.gov.uk

LIST OF PLANNING AUTHORITIES IN ENGLAND AND WALES

Hackney Borough Council	Planning Services, 263 Mare Street, London, E8 3HT; Tel: 020 8356 8062; www.hackney.gov.uk
Hammersmith & Fulham Borough Council	Development Control, 3rd Floor, Town Hall Extension, King Street, Hammersmith, London, W6 9JU; Tel: 020 8753 1081; www.lbhf.gov.uk
Haringey Borough Council	Civic Centre, High Road, Wood Green, London, N22 8LE ; Tel: 020 8489 0000; www.haringey.gov.uk
Harrow Borough Council	Planning Services, Civic Centre, PO Box 37, Station Road, Harrow, HA1 2UY; Tel: 020 8736 6069; www.harrow.gov.uk
Havering Borough Council	Town Hall, Main Road, Romford, RM1 3BB; Tel: 01708 434343; www.havering.gov.uk
Hillingdon Borough Council	Civic Centre, High Street, Uxbridge, UB8 1UW; Tel: 01895 250230; www.hillingdon.gov.uk
Hounslow Borough Council	Borough Planning, The Civic Centre, Lampton Road, Hounslow, TW3 4DN; Tel: 020 8583 2000; www.hounslow.gov.uk
Islington Borough Council	Development Control Service, PO Box 3333, 222 Upper Street, London, N1 1YA; Tel: 020 7527 2000; www.islington.gov.uk
Kensington & Chelsea Borough Council	The Town Hall Hornton Street, London, W8 7NX; Tel: 020 7361 3012; www.rbkc.gov.uk
Kingston upon Thames Borough Council	Guildhall, High Street, Kingston Upon Thames, KT1 1EU; Tel: 020 8547 5330; www.kingston.gov.uk
Lambeth Borough Council	Development Control, Phoenix House, 10 Wandsworth Road, London, SW8 2LL; Tel: 020 7926 1180; www.lambeth.gov.uk
Lewisham Borough Council	Development Control, Planning Services, Laurence House, 1 Catford Road, London, SE6 4SW; Tel: 020 8314 7400; www.lewisham.gov.uk

LIST OF PLANNING AUTHORITIES IN ENGLAND AND WALES

Merton Borough Council	Merton Civic Centre, London Road, Morden, SM4 5DX; Tel: 020 8274 4901; www.merton.gov.uk
Newham Borough Council	Environment & Regeneration Department, Town Hall Annexe, 330–354 Barking Road, East Ham, London, E6 2RT; Tel: 020 8430 2000; www.newham.gov.uk
Redbridge Borough Council	Development Control Section, Planning Services, PO Box 2, Town Hall, 128–142 High Road, Ilford, IG1 1DD; Tel: 020 8554 5000; www.redbridge.gov.uk
Richmond upon Thames Borough Council	Environmental Protection & Customer Services, Civic Centre, 44 York Street, Twickenham, TW1 3BZ; Tel: 0845 612 2660; www.richmond.gov.uk
Southwark Borough Council	Planning and Transport Development Management, PO Box 64529, London, SE1P 5LX; Tel: 020 7525 5403; www.southwark.gov.uk
Sutton Borough Council	Planning, Transportation & Highways, 24 Denmark Road, Carshalton, SM5 2JU; Tel: 020 8770 6200; www.sutton.gov.uk
Tower Hamlets Borough Council	Development & Renewal, Mulberry Place, 5 Clove Crescent, London, E14 1BY; Tel: 020 7364 5009; www.towerhamlets.gov.uk
Waltham Forest Borough Council	Waltham Forest Council, Waltham Forest Town Hall, Forest Road, Walthamstow E17 4JF; Tel: 020 8496 3000; www.walthamforest.gov.uk
Wandsworth Borough Council	Borough Planners Service, The Town Hall, Wandsworth High Street, SW18 2PU; Tel: 020 8871 8871; www.wandsworth.gov.uk
Westminster City Council	Planning and City Development, Westminster City Hall, 64 Victoria Street, London, SW1E 6QP; Tel: 020 7641 2513; www.westminster.gov.uk

LIST OF PLANNING AUTHORITIES IN ENGLAND AND WALES

WALES	
Blaenau Gwent County Borough Council	Planning Department, Council Offices, High Street, Blaina, NP13 3XD; Tel: 01495 355555; www.blaenau-gwent.gov.uk
Bridgend County Borough Council	Planning Department, Civic Offices, Angel Street, Bridgend, CF31 4WB; Tel: 01656 643643; www.bridgend.gov.uk
Caerphilly County Borough Council	Development Control Services, Council Offices, Pontllanfraith, NP12 2YW; Tel: 01443 815588; www.caerphilly.gov.uk
Cardiff County Council	Development Control, Regulatory Services, City Hall, Cathays Park, Cardiff, CF10 3ND; Tel: 029 2087 1134; www.cardiff.gov.uk/dc
Carmarthenshire County Council	County Hall, Carmarthen, SA31 1JP; Tel: 01267 224141; www.carmarthenshire.gov.uk
Ceredigion County Council	Neuadd Cyngor Ceredigion, Penmorfa, Aberaeron, SA46 0PA; Tel: 01545 572 135; www.ceredigion.gov.uk
Conwy County Borough Council	Civic Offices, Colwyn Bay, Conwy, LL29 8AR; Tel: 01492 575245; www.conwy.gov.uk
Denbighshire County Council	Planning Services, Trem Clwyd, Canol-Y-Dre, Ruthin, LL15 1QA; Tel: 01824 706727; www.denbighshire.gov.uk
Flintshire County Council	County Hall, Mold, CH7 6NF; Tel: 01352 703234; www.flintshire.gov.uk
Gwynedd County Council	Environment Directorate, Arfon Area Office, Penrallt, Caernarfon, LL55 1BN; Tel: 01286 682765; www.gwynedd.gov.uk

LIST OF PLANNING AUTHORITIES IN ENGLAND AND WALES

Isle of Anglesey County Council	Development Control Section, Council Offices, Llangefni, Angelsey, LL77 7TW; Tel: 01248 752428; www.anglesey.gov.uk
Merthyr Tydfil County Council	Planning Department Development Control, Ty Keir Hardie, Riverside Court, Avenue de Clichy, Merthyr Tydfil, CF47 8XF; Tel: 01685 726213; www.merthyr.gov.uk
Monmouthshire County Council	Development Control, County Hall, Cwmbran, NP44 2XH; Tel: 01633 844826; www.monmouthshire.gov.uk
Neath & Port Talbot County Council	Neath: Civic Centre, Neath, SA11 3QZ; Tel: 01639 686868 Port Talbot: Civic Centre, Port Talbot, SA13 1PJ; Tel: 01639 686868 www.neath-porttalbot.gov.uk
Newport City Council	Planning Department, Environment & the Economy Section, Civic Centre, Newport, NP9 4UR; Tel: 01633 656656; www.newport.gov.uk
Pembrokeshire County Council	Development Control Department, County Hall, Haverford West, SA61 1TP; Tel: 01437 775324; www.pembrokeshire.gov.uk
Powys County Council	Planning Services, Neuadd Maldwyn, Severn Road, Welshpool, SY21 7AS; Tel: 01938 552828; www.powys.gov.uk
Rhondda Cynnon Taf County Borough Council	Development Control Department, Sardis House, Sardis Road, Pontypridd, CF37 1DU; Tel: 01443 494700 (Environmental Services, Llwyn Castan, Library Road, Pontypridd, CF37 2YA; Tel: 01443 494700); www.rhondda-cynon-taf.gov.uk
Swansea City & Borough Council	County Hall, Oystermouth Road, Swansea, SA1 3SN (Services, Environment Department, The Guildhall, Swansea, SA1 4PH); Tel: 01792 635701; www.swansea.gov.uk

LIST OF PLANNING AUTHORITIES IN ENGLAND AND WALES

Torfaen County Borough Council	Development Control, 4th Floor, County Hall, Cwmbran, NP44 2WN; Tel: 01633 648009; www.torfaen.gov.uk
Vale of Glamorgan Council	Dock Office, Barry Docks, Barry, CF63 4RT; Tel: 01446 704600; www.valeofglamorgan.gov.uk
Wrexham County Borough Council	Planning & Building Control Department, Lambpit Street, Wrexham, LL11 1AR; Tel: 01978 292017; www.wrexham.gov.uk
NATIONAL PARK AUTHORITIES IN ENGLAND AND WALES	
Brecon Beacons National Park	Plas y Ffynnon, Cambrian Way, Brecon, Powys, LD3 7HP; Tel: 01874 624437; www.breconbeacons.org.uk
Broads Authority	Dragonfly House, 2 Gilders Way, Norwich, NR3 1UB; Tel: 01603 610734; www.broads-authority.gov.uk
Dartmoor National Park Authority	Parke, Bovey Tracey, Newton Abbot, Devon, TQ13 9JQ; Tel: 01626 832093; www.dartmoor-npa.gov.uk
Exmoor National Park Authority	Exmoor House, Dulverton, Somerset, TA22 9HL; Tel: 01398 323665; www.exmoor-nationalpark.gov.uk
Lake District National Park Authority	Murley Moss, Oxenholme Road, Kendal, Cumbria, LA9 7RL; Tel: 01539 724555; www.lake-district.gov.uk
New Forest National Park Authority	South Efford House, Milford Road, Everton, Lymington, SO41 0JD; Tel: 01590 646600; www.newforestnpa.gov.uk
Northumberland National Park Authority	Eastburn, South Park, Hexham, Northumberland, NE46 1BS; Tel: 01434 605555; www.northumberlandnationalpark.org.uk
North York Moors National Park Authority	The Old Vicarage, Bondgate, Helmsley, York; YO62 5PB; Tel: 01439 770657; www.visitnorthyorkshiremoors.co.uk
Peak District National Park Authority	Development Control, Aldern House, Baslow Road, Bakewell, DE45 1AE; Tel: 01629 816200; www.peakdistrict.org

LIST OF PLANNING AUTHORITIES IN ENGLAND AND WALES

Pembrokeshire Coast National Park Authority	Development Control Department, Winch Lane, Haverford West, Dyfed, SA61 1PY; Tel: 01646 689076; www.pembrokeshirecoast.org.uk
Snowdonia National Park Authority	Development Control Manager, National Park Office, Penrhyndeudraeth, LL48 6LF; Tel: 01766 770274; www.eryri-npa.gov.uk
Yorkshire Dales National Park Authority	Yoredale, Bainbridge, Leyburn, North Yorkshire, DL8 3EL; Tel: 01969 652345; www.yorkshiredales.org.uk

WHERE CAN I FIND MORE INFORMATION?

Information on *block paving* *manufacturers and guidance on permeable paving*	www.paving.org.uk *or* www.interlay.org.uk *or* www.qpa.org
Information on *rainwater harvesting*	www.ukrha.org
Information on *gardening*	www.rhs.org.uk
Sources to obtain *ordnance survey mapping*	www.promap.co.uk *or* www.plans-online.co.uk *or* www.planningmaps.co.uk *or* www.latitudemapsandglobes.co.uk
Information on *boundary problems*	www.boundary-problems.co.uk
Information on *window and cladding technology*	www.cwct.co.uk
Information on *fire protection*	www.thefpa.co.uk
Information on the *Land Registry*	www.landreg.gov.uk
Information on *glass and glazing*	www.ggf.org.uk

Glossary

Word or phrase	Meaning
advertisement	Includes posters and notices; placards and boards; fascia signs and projecting signs; pole signs and canopy signs; models and devices; advance signs and directional signs; estate agents boards; captive balloon advertising; flags; price markers and price displays; traffic signs and town and village name signs
agricultural holding	The same definition as included in the *Agricultural Holdings Act* 1986
appeal	An appeal that can be lodged under the terms of the 1990 Planning Act against the decision of a council to refuse planning permission; or its failure to determine the application within the statutory time period or any conditions that are imposed on the planning permission issued
area action plan	This is used to provide the planning framework for specific areas within a district or borough where significant change or conservation is needed
area of outstanding natural beauty (AONB)	Areas that are designated under the terms of the *National Parks and Access to the Countryside Act* 1949 as a result of their special landscape character or natural beauty. There are 40 AONBs in England and Wales and nine in Northern Ireland

GLOSSARY

environmental impact assessment (EIA)	A formal process whereby the environmental impacts of a development are systematically assessed to determine whether there will be any unacceptable impacts either during the construction or operational phases
Flat	A separate and self-contained set of premises constructed or adapted for use for the purpose of a dwelling and forming part of a building from some other part of which is divided horizontally
full application	A planning application that contains the full details of the proposed development
gross external area (GEA)	The area of a building measured externally and including all floors. It includes the thickness of the external walls and any external projections
highway	Includes a public road, footpath, bridleway or byway
informal hearing	A method of considering an appeal that allows the case for the council and appellants to be discussed in an open, but informal forum
listed building	A building that is included on a statutory list under the provisions of the *Planning (Listed Buildings and Conservation Areas) Act* 1990 because of its special architectural or historic quality
local development framework (LDF)	Comprises a suite of Local Development Documents, including statutory development plan documents, non-statutory supplementary planning documents, a statement of community involvement, local development scheme and annual monitoring report
local development scheme	A statement of a council's programme for preparing Local Development Documents
local land charges register	A register held by the council recording all charges against a property

GLOSSARY

local planning authority (LPA)	The district or borough council, National Park or Broads authority who has responsibility for determining planning applications and preparing development plans. It does not include county councils in England that have responsibility only for developments involving minerals and waste
local plan	A plan prepared by a district or borough council and comprising a written statement of policies for their area and a map showing specific proposals
material considerations	Any consideration that relates to the use and development of land that requires to be considered in the determination of individual planning applications and appeals
material operation	As defined in section 56(4) of the 1990 Planning Act and means: (a) any work of construction in the course of the erection of a building; (b) the digging of a trench which is to contain the foundations, or part of the foundations, of a building; (c) the laying of any underground main or pipe to the foundations, or part of the foundations, of a building or to any such trench as mentioned in (b) above; (d) the operation in the course of laying out or constructing a road or part of a road; (e) any change in the use of any land which constitutes material development
microgeneration equipment	Equipment used for the generation of electricity or production of any heat which relies mainly on biomass, biofuels, fuel cells, photovoltaics, water (including waves and tides), wind, solar power, geothermal sources, combined heat and power systems and any other source of energy that would cut greenhouse gases and where the capacity would not exceed 50 kilowatts for energy and 45 kilowatts thermal for heat
minor application	A development proposal of less than 10 dwellings

GLOSSARY

national park	An area designated under the *National Parks and Access to the Countryside Act* 1949. There are 15 National Parks in the UK (excluding Northern Ireland), comprising the Brecon Beacons; the Broads; Cairngorms; Dartmoor; Exmoor; Lake District; Loch Lomond; New Forest; Northumberland; North York Moors; Peak District; Pembrokeshire Coastal; Snowdonia; South Downs*; and Yorkshire Dales. (*The South Downs was granted National Park status in March 2009. The new National Park Authority will be set up in 2010 and become fully operational by 2011)
original building	The building that existed on 1 July 1948 or, if the building was built after this date, the building as it was first built
outline application	An application which is submitted to establish the principle of a development proposal and without requiring the submission of full details of the proposal. There is however a need to provide basic information about what is proposed: • the proposed use • the amount of development • an indicative layout • an indication of the upper and lower height, width and length of the proposed building • an indication of where the access points to the site are to be located
owner	A person who owns the land or property or who has a tenancy that has than seven years or more left to run
party wall	The wall or walls that you share with your neighbour if you live in a semi-detached or terraced house or bungalow or flat
permitted development	Development that is permitted by an order issued by the secretary of state and which does not need a separate grant of planning permission

GLOSSARY

planning contravention notice	A formal notice served by the council on the owner or occupier of land requesting information about the use of the land and compliance with conditions attached to a planning permission previously granted
planning inspector	The person appointed by the secretary of state to consider an appeal against a refusal of planning permission or the failure of the council to issue a decision or against conditions imposed by the council on a planning permission, including enforcement, listed building and TPO appeals, etc.
planning inspectorate	A government agency that handles all appeals
planning register	A publicly accessible register held by the council containing information on planning applications that they have received
planning system	The system established by the Planning Acts whereby development is controlled in the main by local planning authorities and where the future needs of the community are planned for through the preparation of development plans
planning policy guidance (PPGs)	Guidance notes that set out the government's policies on different aspects of planning and commonly referred to as PPGs. PPGs cover a wide range of planning matters but are gradually being replaced by PPSs (see below)
planning policy statements (PPSs)	Statements setting out the government's national policies on different aspects of land use planning and commonly referred to as PPSs.
proposals map	A map forming part of the Local Development Plan or Local Development Framework which identifies areas within a council area for protection from development and other land which is allocated for development purposes

GLOSSARY

protected species	Wildlife species that are statutorily protected by law and cannot be disturbed without a prior licence being obtained from Natural England. The protection also extends to the habitats of protected species
public inquiry	A process for considering an appeal where the evidence is provided both in writing and orally and subjected to formal cross-examination
purposes incidental	A use which is subordinate to the main use
regional planning guidance	A document issued by government and setting out the secretary of state's policies for the development and other use of land within a region
regional spatial strategy	A document setting out the secretary of state's policies for the development and other use of land within a region and prepared by regional planning bodies or the equivalent organisation
reserved matters	Matters that are reserved for subsequent approval when an outline planning application is submitted. Reserved Matters comprise: • layout of the development • scale of the buildings in terms of height, width and length • appearance of the building • access to the site and development for pedestrians, cyclists and cars; and • landscaping An outline application can be submitted with one or more of these matters reserved for subsequent approval
restrictive covenant	A private agreement between landowners that can restrict or limit the way that a house, property or land can be used
rights to light	A right to light that has been acquired by 20 years uninterrupted enjoyment of natural daylight or that has been granted to a property owner
satellite dish	An antenna for receiving radio, TV or data communications

GLOSSARY

scheduled ancient monument	An ancient monument that is designated for special protection under the provisions of the *Ancient Monuments and Archaeological Areas Act* 1979
screening opinion	An opinion issued in writing by the council confirming whether a development requires an Environmental Impact Assessment
secretary of state	The secretary of state for communities and local government, who has overall responsibility for the planning system
section 106 agreement	An agreement between a council and any person having an interest in a parcel of land which restricts or regulates the use of the land and can include financial provisions if they are necessary for the purposes of the agreement
site of special scientific interest (SSSI)	A site designated under the *Wildlife and Countryside Act* 1981 because of its wildlife and geological importance. There are 4,000 designated SSSIs in England.
site specific allocations	A document prepared by the council as part of the Local Development Framework which identifies sites for specific uses
stop notice	A formal notice issued by the council requiring that an unauthorised use or activity should cease before an Enforcement Notice takes effect
supplementary planning documents (SPDs)	Documents prepared by the council as part of their Local Development Framework and subject to consultation, but which do not form part of the statutory development plan
statement of community involvement	A document prepared by the council as part of the Local Development Framework and which sets out how the local community will be consulted in the preparation and review of development plan documents and individual planning applications
statutory consultations	Consultations that a council is legally obliged to carry out prior to determining a planning application

GLOSSARY

temporary stop notice	A formal notice issued by the council requiring that an unauthorised use or activity should cease immediately
terrace house	A terrace house means a house situated in a row of three or more houses that is used or designed as a single house and where: • the party wall is shared with, or has a main wall adjoining the main wall of a house on either side; or • if it is at the end of a row, the house has a party wall shared with a house that shares its main wall with a house on either side
the 'Broads'	The Norfolk and Suffolk Broads. Confirmation on the extent of the 'Broads' can be obtained at www.broads-authority.gov.uk. The Broads has the same status as a National Park
tree preservation order (TPO)	An order made by the council which makes it an offence to cut down, top, lop, uproot, wilfully damage or wilfully destroy a tree without the council's prior consent. An order can relate to an individual tree or a group of trees
unitary development plan (UDP)	A development plan prepared under the terms of the 1990 Planning Act and comprising two parts: (1) a written statement setting out the council's general policies for the development and other use of land within the area; and (2) a written statement together with maps, diagrams, illustrations and reasoned justification confirming the detailed proposals for development and the other use of land

GLOSSARY

use class	The classification of a building according to its use. Different uses for buildings are categorised on the basis of their similarity, e.g. shops, restaurants, dwellings, etc. There are 14 different Use Classes in total. Dwellings are categorised as Use Class C3. Changing from one use to another use within the same Use Class is Permitted Development
world heritage site	A property that appears on the World Heritage List which is kept under article 11(2) of the 1972 UNESCO Convention for the Protection of the World Cultural and Natural Heritage. Details of these sites can be obtained from whc.unesco.org
written representations	The process whereby an appeal proceeds on the basis of a written exchange of arguments only

Abbreviations

Abbreviation	Meaning
AONB	area of outstanding natural beauty
DPD	development plan document
EIA	environmental impact assessment
GEA	gross external area
LDD	local development document
LDF	local development framework
LPA	local planning authority
PINS	planning inspectorate notification service
PPGs	planning policy guidance notes
PPSs	planning policy statements
RPG	regional planning guidance
RSS	regional spatial strategy
SPD	supplementary planning document
SI	statutory instrument
TPO	tree preservation order
UDP	unitary development plan

PLANNING APPLICATION FORMS

Planning and Development
Ashford Borough Council, Civic Centre, Tannery Lane, Ashford, Kent TN23 1PL

Email: planning.enquiries@ashford.gov.uk
Telephone: 01233 330264
Website: www.ashford.gov.uk

Householder Application for Planning Permission for works or extension to a dwelling.
Town and Country Planning Act 1990

Publication of planning applications on council websites

Please note that with the exception of applicant contact details and Certificates of Ownership, the information provided on this application form and in supporting documents may be published on the council's website.

If you have provided any other information as part of your application which falls within the definition of personal data under the Data Protection Act which you do not wish to be published on the council's website, please contact the council's planning department.

Please complete using block capitals and black ink.
It is important that you read the accompanying guidance notes as incorrect completion will delay the processing of your application.

1. Applicant Name and Address

Title:
First name:
Last name:
Company (optional):
Unit:
House number:
House suffix:
House name:
Address 1:
Address 2:
Address 3:
Town:
County:
Country:
Postcode:

2. Agent Name and Address

Title:
First name:
Last name:
Company (optional):
Unit:
House number:
House suffix:
House name:
Address 1:
Address 2:
Address 3:
Town:
County:
Country:
Postcode:

3. Description of Proposed Works

Please describe the proposed works:

PLANNING APPLICATION FORMS

3. Description of Proposed Works (continued)

Has the work already started? ☐ Yes ☐ No

If Yes, please state when the work was started (DD/MM/YYYY): [_____] (date must be pre-application submission)

Has the work already been completed? ☐ Yes ☐ No

If Yes, please state when the work was completed (DD/MM/YYYY): [_____] (date must be pre-application submission)

4. Site Address Details

Please provide the full postal address of the application site.

Unit: [____] House number: [____] House suffix: [____]

House name: [____]

Address 1: [____]

Address 2: [____]

Address 3: [____]

Town: [____]

County: [____]

Postcode (optional): [____]

5. Pedestrian and Vehicle Access, Roads and Rights of Way

Is a new or altered vehicle access proposed to or from the public highway? ☐ Yes ☐ No

Is a new or altered pedestrian access proposed to or from the public highway? ☐ Yes ☐ No

Do the proposals require any diversions, extinguishments and/or creation of public rights of way? ☐ Yes ☐ No

If Yes to any questions, please show details on your plans or drawings and state the reference number(s) of the plan(s)/drawing(s):

6. Pre-application Advice

Has assistance or prior advice been sought from the local authority about this application? ☐ Yes ☐ No

If Yes, please complete the following information about the advice you were given. (This will help the authority to deal with this application more efficiently).
Please tick if the full contact details are not known, and then complete as much possible: ☐

Officer name:

Reference:

Date (DD MM YYYY): [____]
(must be pre-application submission)

Details of the pre-application advice received:

7. Trees and Hedges

Are there any trees or hedges on your own property or on adjoining properties which are within falling distance of your boundary? ☐ Yes ☐ No

If Yes, please mark their position on a scaled plan and state the reference number of any plans or drawings:

Will any trees or hedges need to be removed or pruned in order to carry out your proposal? ☐ Yes ☐ No

If Yes, please show on your plans which trees by giving them numbers e.g. T1, T2 etc, state the reference number of the plan(s)/drawing(s) and indicate the scale.

8. Parking

Will the proposed works affect existing car parking arrangements? ☐ Yes ☐ No

If Yes, please describe:

9. Council Employee / Member

Is the applicant or agent related to any member of staff or elected member of the council? ☐ Yes ☐ No

If Yes, please provide details:

10. Materials

If applicable, please state what materials are to be used externally. Include type, colour and name for each material:

	Existing (where applicable)	Proposed	Not applicable	Don't Know	Drawing references if applicable
Walls			☐	☐	
Roof			☐	☐	
Windows			☐	☐	
Doors			☐	☐	
Boundary treatments (e.g. fences, walls)			☐	☐	
Vehicle access and hard-standing			☐	☐	
Lighting			☐	☐	
Others (please specify)			☐	☐	

Are you supplying additional information on submitted plan(s)/drawing(s)/design and access statement? ☐ Yes ☐ No

If Yes, please state references for the plan(s)/drawing(s)/design and access statement:

PLANNING APPLICATION FORMS

11. Certificates

One Certificate A, B, C, or D, must be completed, together with the Agricultural Holdings Certificate with this application form

CERTIFICATE OF OWNERSHIP - CERTIFICATE A
Town and Country Planning (General Development Procedure) Order 1995 Certificate under Article 7

I certify/The applicant certifies that on the day 21 days before the date of this application nobody except myself/ the applicant was the owner *(owner is a person with a freehold interest or leasehold interest with at least 7 years left to run)* of any part of the land or building to which the application relates.

Signed - Applicant: Or signed - Agent: Date (DD/MM/YYYY):

CERTIFICATE OF OWNERSHIP - CERTIFICATE B
Town and Country Planning (General Development Procedure) Order 1995 Certificate under Article 7

I certify/ The applicant certifies that I have/the applicant has given the requisite notice to everyone else (as listed below) who, on the day 21 days before the date of this application, was the owner *(owner is a person with a freehold interest or leasehold interest with at least 7 years left to run)* of any part of the land or building to which this application relates.

Name of Owner	Address	Date Notice Served

Signed - Applicant: Or signed - Agent: Date (DD/MM/YYYY):

CERTIFICATE OF OWNERSHIP - CERTIFICATE C
Town and Country Planning (General Development Procedure) Order 1995 Certificate under Article 7

I certify/ The applicant certifies that:
- Neither Certificate A or B can be issued for this application
- All reasonable steps have been taken to find out the names and addresses of the other owners *(owner is a person with a freehold interest or leasehold interest with at least 7 years left to run)* of the land or building, or of a part of it , but I have/ the applicant has been unable to do so.

The steps taken were:

Name of Owner	Address	Date Notice Served

Notice of the application has been published in the following newspaper (circulating in the area where the land is situated):

On the following date (which must not be earlier than 21 days before the date of the application):

Signed - Applicant: Or signed - Agent: Date (DD/MM/YYYY):

11. Certificates (continued)

CERTIFICATE OF OWNERSHIP - CERTIFICATE D
Town and Country Planning (General Development Procedure) Order 1995 Certificate under Article 7

I certify/ The applicant certifies that:
- Certificate A cannot be issued for this application
- All reasonable steps have been taken to find out the names and addresses of everyone else who, on the day 21 days before the date of this application, was the owner (*owner is a person with a freehold interest or leasehold interest with at least 7 years left to run*) of any part of the land to which this application relates, but I have/ the applicant has been unable to do so.

The steps taken were:

Notice of the application has been published in the following newspaper (circulating in the area where the land is situated):

On the following date (which must not be earlier than 21 days before the date of the application):

Signed - Applicant: Or signed - Agent: Date (DD/MM/YYYY):

AGRICULTURAL HOLDINGS CERTIFICATE
Town and Country Planning (General Development Procedure) Order 1995 Certificate under Article 7

Agricultural Land Declaration - You Must Complete Either A or B

(A) None of the land to which the application relates is, or is part of, an agricultural holding.

Signed - Applicant: Or signed - Agent: Date (DD/MM/YYYY):

B) I have/ The applicant has given the requisite notice to every person other than myself/ the applicant who, on the day 21 days before the date of this application, was a tenant of an agricultural holding on all or part of the land to which this application relates, as listed below:

Name of Tenant	Address	Date Notice Served

Signed - Applicant: Or signed - Agent: Date (DD/MM/YYYY):

12. Planning Application Requirements - Checklist

Please read the following checklist to make sure you have sent all the information in support of your proposal. Failure to submit all information required will result in your application being deemed invalid. It will not be considered valid until all information required by the Local Planning Authority has been submitted.

- The original and 3 copies of a completed and dated application form: ☐
- The original and 3 copies of a plan which identifies the land to which the application relates drawn to an identified scale and showing the direction of North: ☐
- The original and 3 copies of other plans and drawings or information necessary to describe the subject of the application: ☐
- The original and 3 copies of a design and access statement where proposed works fall within one of the following designated areas: ☐
  - National Park
  - Site of special scientific interest
  - Conservation area
  - Area of outstanding natural beauty
  - World Heritage Site
  - The Broads
- The correct fee: ☐
- The original and 3 copies of the completed, dated Article 7 Certificate (Agricultural Holdings): ☐
- The original and 3 copies of the completed, dated Ownership Certificate (A, B, C or D - as applicable): ☐

13. Declaration

I/we hereby apply for planning permission/consent as described in this form and the accompanying plans/drawings and additional information.

Signed - Applicant: Or signed - Agent: Date (DD/MM/YYYY):   (date cannot be pre-application)

PLANNING APPLICATION FORMS

14. Applicant Contact Details

Telephone numbers

Country code: National number: Extension number:

Country code: Mobile number (optional):

Country code: Fax number (optional):

Email address (optional):

15. Agent Contact Details

Telephone numbers

Country code: National number: Extension number:

Country code: Mobile number (optional):

Country code: Fax number (optional):

Email address (optional):

16. Site Visit

Can the site be seen from a public road, public footpath, bridleway or other public land? ☐ Yes ☐ No

If the planning authority needs to make an appointment to carry out a site visit, whom should they contact? *(Please select only one)* ☐ Agent ☐ Applicant ☐ Other (if different from the agent/applicant's details)

If Other has been selected, please provide:

Contact name:

Telephone number:

Email address:

PLANNING APPLICATION FORMS

Planning and Development
Ashford Borough Council, Civic Centre, Tannery Lane, Ashford, Kent TN23 1PL

Email: planning.enquiries@ashford.gov.uk
Telephone: 01233 330264
Website: www.ashford.gov.uk

Householder Application for Planning Permission for works or extension to a dwelling and conservation area consent.
Town and Country Planning Act 1990
Planning (Listed Buildings and Conservation Areas Act) 1990

Publication of planning applications on council websites
Please note that with the exception of applicant contact details and Certificates of Ownership, the information provided on this application form and in supporting documents may be published on the council's website.

If you have provided any other information as part of your application which falls within the definition of personal data under the Data Protection Act which you do not wish to be published on the council's website, please contact the council's planning department.

Please complete using block capitals and black ink.
It is important that you read the accompanying guidance notes as incorrect completion will delay the processing of your application.

1. Applicant Name and Address

Field		Field	
Title:		First name:	
Last name:			
Company (optional):			
Unit:		House number:	House suffix:
House name:			
Address 1:			
Address 2:			
Address 3:			
Town:			
County:			
Country:			
Postcode:			

2. Agent Name and Address

Field		Field	
Title:		First name:	
Last name:			
Company (optional):			
Unit:		House number:	House suffix:
House name:			
Address 1:			
Address 2:			
Address 3:			
Town:			
County:			
Country:			
Postcode:			

3. Description of Proposed Works

Please describe the proposed works:

PLANNING APPLICATION FORMS

3. Description of Proposed Works (continued)

Has the work already started? ☐ Yes ☐ No

If Yes, please state when the work was started (DD/MM/YYYY): [____] (date must be pre-application submission)

Has the work been completed? ☐ Yes ☐ No

If Yes, please state when the work was completed (DD/MM/YYYY): [____] (date must be pre-application submission)

4. Site Address Details

Please provide the full postal address of the application site.

Unit: [____]
House number: [____]
House suffix: [____]
House name: [____]
Address 1: [____]
Address 2: [____]
Address 3: [____]
Town: [____]
County: [____]
Postcode (optional): [____]

Description of location or a grid reference.
(must be completed if postcode is not known):

Easting: [____] Northing: [____]

Description:

5. Pre-application Advice

Has assistance or prior advice been sought from the local authority about this application? ☐ Yes ☐ No

If Yes, please complete the following information about the advice you were given. (This will help the authority to deal with this application more efficiently).
Please tick if the full contact details are not known, and then complete as much as possible: ☐

Officer name:

Reference:

Date (DD/MM/YYYY):
(must be pre-application submission) [____]

Details of the pre-application advice received:

6. Pedestrian and Vehicle Access, Roads and Rights of Way

Is a new or altered vehicle access proposed to or from the public highway? ☐ Yes ☐ No

Is a new or altered pedestrian access proposed to or from the public highway? ☐ Yes ☐ No

Do the proposals require any diversions, extinguishments and/or creation of public rights of way? ☐ Yes ☐ No

If Yes to any questions, please show details on your plans or drawings and state the reference number(s) of the plan(s)/drawing(s)

7. Trees and Hedges

Are there any trees or hedges on your own property or on adjoining properties which are within falling distance of your boundary? ☐ Yes ☐ No

If Yes, please mark their position on a scaled plan and state the reference number of any plan(s)/drawing(s):

Will any trees or hedges need to be removed or pruned in order to carry out your proposal? ☐ Yes ☐ No

If Yes, please show on your plans which trees by giving them numbers e.g. T1, T2 etc, state the reference number of the plan(s)/drawing(s) and indicate the scale.

PLANNING APPLICATION FORMS

8. Parking

Will the proposed works affect existing car parking arrangements? ☐ Yes ☐ No

If Yes, please describe:

9. Council Employee / Member

Is the applicant or agent related to any member of staff or elected member of the council? ☐ Yes ☐ No

If Yes, please provide details:

10. Materials

If applicable, please state what materials are to be used externally. Include type, colour and name for each material:

	Existing (where applicable)	Proposed	Not applicable	Don't Know	Drawing references if applicable
Walls			☐	☐	
Roof			☐	☐	
Windows			☐	☐	
Doors			☐	☐	
Boundary treatments (e.g. fences, walls)			☐	☐	
Vehicle access and hard-standing			☐	☐	
Lighting			☐	☐	
Others (please specify)			☐	☐	

Are you supplying additional information on submitted plan(s)/drawing(s)/design and access statement? ☐ Yes ☐ No

If Yes, please state references for the plan(s)/drawing(s)/design and access statement:

11. Explanation For Proposed Demolition Work

Why is it necessary to demolish all or part of the building(s) and or structure(s)?

PLANNING APPLICATION FORMS

15. Applicant Contact Details

Telephone numbers

Country code: | National number: | Extension number:

Country code: | Mobile number (optional):

Country code: | Fax number (optional):

Email address (optional):

16. Agent Contact Details

Telephone numbers

Country code: | National number: | Extension number:

Country code: | Mobile number (optional):

Country code: | Fax number (optional):

Email address (optional):

17. Site Visit

Can the site be seen from a public road, public footpath, bridleway or other public land? ☐ Yes ☐ No

If the planning authority needs to make an appointment to carry out a site visit, whom should they contact? *(Please select only one)* ☐ Agent ☐ Applicant ☐ Other (if different from the agent/applicant's details)

If Other has been selected, please provide:

Contact name: | Telephone number:

Email address:

PLANNING APPLICATION FORMS

Planning and Development
Ashford Borough Council, Civic Centre, Tannery Lane, Ashford, Kent TN23 1PL

Email: planning.enquiries@ashford.gov.uk
Telephone: 01233 330264
Website: www.ashford.gov.uk

Householder Application for Planning Permission for works or extension to a dwelling and listed building consent.
Town and Country Planning Act 1990

Publication of planning applications on council websites
Please note that with the exception of applicant contact details and Certificates of Ownership, the information provided on this application form and in supporting documents may be published on the council's website.

If you have provided any other information as part of your application which falls within the definition of personal data under the Data Protection Act which you do not wish to be published on the council's website, please contact the council's planning department.

Please complete using block capitals and black ink.
It is important that you read the accompanying guidance notes as incorrect completion will delay the processing of your application.

1. Applicant Name and Address

Field	
Title:	First name:
Last name:	
Company (optional):	
Unit:	House number: / House suffix:
House name:	
Address 1:	
Address 2:	
Address 3:	
Town:	
County:	
Country:	
Postcode:	

2. Agent Name and Address

Field	
Title:	First name:
Last name:	
Company (optional):	
Unit:	House number: / House suffix:
House name:	
Address 1:	
Address 2:	
Address 3:	
Town:	
County:	
Country:	
Postcode:	

3. Description of Proposed Works

Please describe the proposed works:

219

PLANNING APPLICATION FORMS

3. Description of Proposed Works (continued)

Has the work already started? ☐ Yes ☐ No

If Yes, please state when the work was started (DD/MM/YYYY): [____] (date must be pre-application submission)

Has the work already been completed? ☐ Yes ☐ No

If Yes, please state when the work was completed (DD/MM/YYYY): [____] (date must be pre-application submission)

4. Site Address Details

Please provide the full postal address of the application site.

Unit: [____]　House number: [____]　House suffix: [____]

House name: [____]

Address 1: [____]

Address 2: [____]

Address 3: [____]

Town: [____]

County: [____]

Postcode (optional): [____]

Description of location or a grid reference.
(must be completed if postcode is not known):

Easting: [____]　Northing: [____]

Description:
[____]

5. Pre-application Advice

Has assistance or prior advice been sought from the local authority about this application? ☐ Yes ☐ No

If Yes, please complete the following information about the advice you were given. (This will help the authority to deal with this application more efficiently).
Please tick if the full contact details are not known, and then complete as much as possible: ☐

Officer name: [____]

Reference: [____]

Date (DD/MM/YYYY): [____]
(must be pre-application submission)

Details of pre-application advice received?
[____]

6. Pedestrian and Vehicle Access, Roads and Rights of Way

Is a new or altered vehicle access proposed to or from the public highway? ☐ Yes ☐ No

Is a new or altered pedestrian access proposed to or from the public highway? ☐ Yes ☐ No

Do the proposals require any diversions, extinguishments and/or creation of public rights of way? ☐ Yes ☐ No

If Yes to any questions, please show details on your plans or drawings and state the reference number(s) of the plan(s)/drawing(s)
[____]

7. Trees and Hedges

Are there any trees or hedges on your own property or on adjoining properties which are within falling distance of your boundary? ☐ Yes ☐ No

If Yes, please mark their position on a scaled plan and state the reference number of any plan(s)/drawing(s):
[____]

Will any trees or hedges need to be removed or pruned in order to carry out your proposal? ☐ Yes ☐ No

If Yes, please show on your plans which trees by giving them numbers e.g. T1, T2 etc, state the reference number of the plan(s)/drawing(s) and indicate the scale.
[____]

$Date: 2008/05/16 13:01:00 $ $Revision: 1.28 $

8. Materials

Please provide a description of existing and proposed materials and finishes to be used in the building (demolition excluded):

	Existing (where applicable)	Proposed	Not applicable	Don't Know
External walls			☐	☐
Roof covering			☐	☐
Chimney			☐	☐
Windows			☐	☐
External doors			☐	☐
Ceilings			☐	☐
Internal walls			☐	☐
Floors			☐	☐
Internal doors			☐	☐
Rainwater goods			☐	☐
Boundary treatments (e.g. fences, walls)			☐	☐
Vehicle access and hard standing			☐	☐
Lighting			☐	☐
Others (add description)			☐	☐

Are you supplying additional information on submitted drawings or plans? ☐ Yes ☐ No

If Yes, please state plan(s)/drawing(s) references:

PLANNING APPLICATION FORMS

9. Demolition

Does the proposal include the partial or total demolition of a listed building? ☐ Yes ☐ No

If Yes, which of the following does the proposal involve?

a) Total demolition of the listed building: ☐ Yes ☐ No

b) Demolition of a building within the curtilage of the listed building: ☐ Yes ☐ No

c) Demolition of a part of the listed building: ☐ Yes ☐ No

If the answer to c) is Yes:

i) What is the total volume of the listed building?(cubic metres)	
ii) What is the volume of the part to be demolished?(cubic metres)	
iii) What was the (approximate) date of the erection of the part to be removed? (MM/YYYY) (date must be pre-application submission)	

Please provide a brief description of the building or part of the building you are proposing to demolish:

Why is it necessary to demolish or extend (as applicable) all or part of the building(s) and or structure(s)?

10. Listed Building Alterations

Do the proposed works include alterations to a listed building? ☐ Yes ☐ No

If Yes, do the proposed works include: (you must answer each of the questions)

a) Works to the interior of the building? ☐ Yes ☐ No

b) Works to the exterior of the building? ☐ Yes ☐ No

c) Works to any structure or object fixed to the property (or buildings within its curtilage) internally or externally? ☐ Yes ☐ No

d) Stripping out of any internal wall, ceiling or floor finishes (e.g. plaster, floorboards)? ☐ Yes ☐ No

If the answer to any of these questions is Yes, please provide plans, drawings, photographs sufficient to identify the location, extent and character of the items to be removed, and the proposal for their replacement, including any new means of structural support and state references for the plan(s)/drawing(s):

11. Listed Building Grading

Please state the grading (if known) of the building in the list of Buildings of Special Architectural or Historic interest? (Note: only one box must be ticked)

Grade I ☐   Ecclesiastical Grade I ☐

Grade II* ☐   Ecclesiastical Grade II* ☐

Grade II ☐   Ecclesiastical Grade II ☐

                   Don't know ☐

12. Immunity From Listing

Has a Certificate of Immunity from Listing been sought in respect of this building?
☐ Yes   ☐ No   ☐ Don't know

If Yes, please provide the result of the application:

13. Parking

Will the proposed works affect existing car parking arrangements? ☐ Yes ☐ No

If Yes, please describe:

14. Council Employee / Member

Is the applicant or agent related to any member of staff or elected member of the council? ☐ Yes ☐ No

If Yes, please provide details:

15. Certificates

One certificate A, B, C, or D must be completed, together with the Agricultural Holdings Certificate with this application form

CERTIFICATE OF OWNERSHIP - CERTIFICATE A
Certificate under Article 7 of the Town and Country Planning (General Development Procedure) Order 1995 & Regulation 6 of the Planning (Listed Buildings and Conservation Areas) Regulations 1990

I certify/The applicant certifies that on the day 21 days before the date of this application nobody except myself/ the applicant was the owner *(owner is a person with a freehold interest or leasehold interest with at least 7 years left to run)* of any part of the land or building to which the application relates.

Signed - Applicant:	Or signed - Agent:	Date (DD/MM/YYYY):

CERTIFICATE OF OWNERSHIP - CERTIFICATE B
Certificate under Article 7 of the Town and Country Planning (General Development Procedure) Order 1995 & Regulation 6 of the Planning (Listed Buildings and Conservation Areas) Regulations 1990

I certify/ The applicant certifies that I have/the applicant has given the requisite notice to everyone else (as listed below) who, on the day 21 days before the date of this application, was the owner *(owner is a person with a freehold interest or leasehold interest with at least 7 years left to run)* of any part of the land or building to which this application relates.

Name of Owner	Address	Date Notice Served

Signed - Applicant:	Or signed - Agent:	Date (DD/MM/YYYY):

CERTIFICATE OF OWNERSHIP - CERTIFICATE C
Certificate under Article 7 of the Town and Country Planning (General Development Procedure) Order 1995 & Regulation 6 of the Planning (Listed Buildings and Conservation Areas) Regulations 1990

I certify/ The applicant certifies that:
- Neither Certificate A or B can be issued for this application
- All reasonable steps have been taken to find out the names and addresses of the other owners *(owner is a person with a freehold interest or leasehold interest with at least 7 years left to run)* of the land or building, or of a part of it , but I have/ the applicant has been unable to do so.

The steps taken were:

Name of Owner	Address	Date Notice Served

Notice of the application has been published in the following newspaper (circulating in the area where the land is situated):	On the following date (which must not be earlier than 21 days before the date of the application):

Signed - Applicant:	Or signed - Agent:	Date (DD/MM/YYYY):

PLANNING APPLICATION FORMS

15. Certificates (continued)

CERTIFICATE OF OWNERSHIP - CERTIFICATE D
Certificate under Article 7 of the Town and Country Planning (General Development Procedure) Order 1995 & Regulation 6 of the Planning (Listed Buildings and Conservation Areas) Regulations 1990

I certify/ The applicant certifies that:
- Certificate A cannot be issued for this application
- All reasonable steps have been taken to find out the names and addresses of everyone else who, on the day 21 days before the date of this application, was the owner *(owner is a person with a freehold interest or leasehold interest with at least 7 years left to run)* of any part of the land to which this application relates, but I have/ the applicant has been unable to do so.

The steps taken were:

Notice of the application has been published in the following newspaper (circulating in the area where the land is situated):	On the following date (which must not be earlier than 21 days before the date of the application):

Signed - Applicant:	Or signed - Agent:	Date (DD/MM/YYYY):

AGRICULTURAL HOLDINGS CERTIFICATE
Town and Country Planning (General Development Procedure) Order 1995 Certificate under Article 7

Agricultural Land Declaration - You Must Complete Either A or B

(A) None of the land to which the application relates is, or is part of, an agricultural holding.

Signed - Applicant:	Or signed - Agent:	Date (DD/MM/YYYY):

(B) I have/ The applicant has given the requisite notice to every person other than myself/ the applicant who, on the day 21 days before the date of this application, was a tenant of an agricultural holding on all or part of the land to which this application relates, as listed below:

Name of Tenant	Address	Date Notice Served

Signed - Applicant:	Or signed - Agent:	Date (DD/MM/YYYY):

16. Planning Application Requirements - Checklist

Please read the following checklist to make sure you have sent all the information in support of your proposal. Failure to submit all information required will result in your application being deemed invalid. It will not be considered valid until all information required by the Local Planning Authority has been submitted.

- The original and 3 copies of a completed and dated application form: ☐
- The original and 3 copies of a plan which identifies the land to which the application relates drawn to an identified scale and showing the direction of North: ☐
- The original and 3 copies of other plans and drawings or information necessary to describe the subject of the application: ☐
- The original and 3 copies of a design and access statement where proposed works fall within one of the following designated areas:
  - National Park
  - Site of special scientific interest
  - Conservation area
  - Area of outstanding natural beauty
  - World Heritage Site
  - The Broads ☐
- The correct fee: ☐
- The original and 3 copies of the completed, dated Article 7 Certificate (Agricultural Holdings): ☐
- The original and 3 copies of the completed, dated Ownership Certificate (A, B, C or D - as applicable): ☐

17. Declaration

I/we hereby apply for planning permission/consent as described in this form and the accompanying plans/drawings and additional information.

Signed - Applicant:	Or signed - Agent:	Date (DD/MM/YYYY):
		(date cannot be pre-application)

PLANNING APPLICATION FORMS

18. Applicant Contact Details

Telephone numbers

Country code: ____ National number: ____ Extension number: ____

Country code: ____ Mobile number (optional): ____

Country code: ____ Fax number (optional): ____

Email address (optional): ____

19. Agent Contact Details

Telephone numbers

Country code: ____ National number: ____ Extension number: ____

Country code: ____ Mobile number (optional): ____

Country code: ____ Fax number (optional): ____

Email address (optional): ____

20. Site Visit

Can the site be seen from a public road, public footpath, bridleway or other public land? ☐ Yes ☐ No

If the planning authority needs to make an appointment to carry out a site visit, whom should they contact? *(Please select only one)* ☐ Agent ☐ Applicant ☐ Other (if different from the agent/applicant's details)

If Other has been selected, please provide:

Contact name: ____

Telephone number: ____

Email address: ____

PLANNING APPLICATION FORMS

The Planning Inspectorate

Further information about us and the planning appeal system is available on our website
www.planning-inspectorate.gov.uk

PLANNING APPEAL

For official use only
Date Received

If you need this document in large print, on audio tape, in Braille or in another language, please contact our helpline on 0117 372 6372.

Please use a separate form for each appeal

Your appeal and essential supporting documents must reach the Inspectorate within 6 months of the date shown on the Local Planning Authority's decision notice (or, for 'failure' appeals, within 6 months of the date by which they should have decided the application).

Before completing this form, please read our booklet 'Making your planning appeal' which was sent to you with this form.

WARNING: If any of the 'Essential supporting documents' listed in Section J are not received by us within the 6 month period, the appeal will not be accepted.

PLEASE PRINT CLEARLY IN CAPITALS USING BLACK INK

A. APPELLANT DETAILS

The name of the person(s) making the appeal must appear as an applicant on the planning application form.

Name

Organisation Name (if applicable)

Address

Postcode

Daytime Tel   Fax

Email

I prefer to be contacted by   Email   Post

B. AGENT DETAILS (if any) FOR THE APPEAL

Name

Organisation Name (if applicable)

Address

Postcode

Your Ref

Daytime Tel   Fax

Email

I prefer to be contacted by   Email   Post

C. LOCAL PLANNING AUTHORITY (LPA) DETAILS

Name of the LPA

LPA's application reference no.

Date of the planning application

Date of LPA's decision notice (if issued)

PINS PF01 (REVISED MARCH 2005)   Please turn over

PLANNING APPLICATION FORMS

The Planning Inspectorate - Planning Appeal

D. APPEAL SITE ADDRESS

Address

Postcode   Note: Failure to provide the full postcode may delay the processing of your appeal.

Is the appeal site within a Green Belt?   YES   NO

E. DESCRIPTION OF THE DEVELOPMENT

Please enter details of the proposed development. This should normally be taken from the planning application form, but if the application was revised (and agreed) while it was with the local planning authority for consideration, you may enter a description of the revised scheme.

Size of the whole appeal site (in hectares)

Area of floor space of proposed development (in square metres)

Has the description of the development changed from that entered on the application form?   YES   NO

F. REASON FOR THE APPEAL

This appeal is against the decision of the LPA to: *Please tick ONE box only* ✓

1	Refuse planning permission for the development described in Section E.	1
2	Grant planning permission for the development subject to conditions to which you object.	2
3	Refuse approval of the matters reserved under an outline planning permission.	3
4	Grant approval of the matters reserved under an outline planning permission subject to conditions to which you object.	4
5	Refuse to approve any matter required by a condition on a previous planning permission (other than those in 3 or 4 above).	5
	OR	
6	The failure of the LPA to give notice of its decision within the appropriate period (usually 8 weeks) on an application for permission or approval.	6

227

PLANNING APPLICATION FORMS

G. CHOICE OF PROCEDURE

CHOOSE ONE PROCEDURE ONLY

You should start by reading our booklet 'Making your planning appeal' which explains the different procedures used to determine planning appeals. In short there are 3 possible methods: - written representations, hearings and inquiries. You should consider carefully which method suits your circumstances.

Please note that when we decide how the appeal will proceed we will take into account the LPA's views. ✓

1 WRITTEN REPRESENTATIONS

This is normally the simplest, quickest and most straightforward way of making an appeal. Three out of every four people making an appeal choose this method. The written procedure is particularly suited to small-scale developments (e.g. extensions of buildings, individual houses or small groups of houses, appeals against conditions and changes of use). It is also very popular with people making their own appeal without professional help. The process involves the submission of written 'grounds of appeal' followed by a written statement and any supporting documents. It also provides an opportunity to comment in writing on the Local Planning Authority's reasons for refusing permission (or failing to determine the application). An Inspector will study all of the documents before visiting the appeal site/area and issuing a written decision.

NOTE: The Inspector will visit the site <u>unaccompanied</u> by either party unless the relevant part of the site cannot be seen from a road or other public land, or it is essential for the Inspector to enter the site to check measurements or other relevant facts.

a) If the written procedure is agreed, can the relevant part of the appeal site be seen from a road, public foopath, bridleway or other public land?   YES / NO

b) Is it essential for the Inspector to enter the site to check measurements or other relevant facts?   YES / NO

If the answer to **1b** is 'YES' please explain

2 HEARINGS

This process is likely to be suited to slightly more complicated cases which require detailed discussion about the merits of a proposal. Like the written procedure, the process starts with the submission of 'written grounds of appeal' followed by a full written statement of case and an opportunity to comment in writing on the Local Planning Authority's reasons for refusing permission (or failing to determine the application). The Planning Inspectorate will then arrange a hearing at which the Local Planning Authority and the appellant(s) will be represented. Members of the public, interested bodies (e.g. Parish/Town Councils) and the press may also attend. At the hearing the Inspector will lead a discussion on the matters already presented in the written statements and supporting documents. The Inspector will visit the site/area and issue a written decision in the same way as the written procedure.

Although you may prefer a hearing the Inspectorate must consider your appeal suitable for this procedure.

3 INQUIRIES

This is the most formal of procedures. Although it is not a court of law the proceedings will often seem to be quite similar as the parties to the appeal will usually be legally represented and expert witnesses will be called to give evidence. Members of the public and press may also attend. In general, inquiries are suggested for appeals that:

- are complex and particularly controversial;
- have caused a lot of local interest;
- involve the need to question evidence through formal cross-examination.

PLANNING APPLICATION FORMS

H. GROUNDS OF APPEAL

If you have requested the written procedure, please provide your **FULL** grounds of appeal.

If you have requested a hearing or an inquiry, you do not have to provide your full grounds of appeal. You can provide only a brief outline of your grounds, but it must be sufficiently detailed and comprehensive to enable the LPA to prepare their case.

Refer to our booklet 'Making your planning appeal' for help.

Please continue on a separate sheet if necessary.

229

PLANNING APPLICATION FORMS

H. GROUNDS OF APPEAL (continued)

PLANNING APPLICATION FORMS

I. APPEAL SITE OWNERSHIP DETAILS

We need to know who owns the appeal site. If you do not own the appeal site or if you own only a part of it, we need to know the name(s) of the owner(s) or part owner(s). We also need to be sure that any other owner knows that you have made an appeal.
YOU MUST TICK WHICH OF THE CERTIFICATES APPLIES.

Please read the enclosed *Guidance Notes* if in doubt.

Please tick ONE box only ✓

If you are the <u>sole</u> owner of the <u>whole</u> appeal site, certificate A will apply:

CERTIFICATE A   A

I certify that, on the day 21 days before the date of this appeal, nobody except the appellant, was the owner (see Note (i) of the *Guidance Notes* for a definition) of any part of the land to which the appeal relates:

OR

CERTIFICATE B   B

I certify that the appellant (or the agent) has given the requisite notice (see *Guidance Notes*) to everyone else who, on the day 21 days before the date of this appeal, was the owner (see Note (i) of the Guidance Notes for a definition) of any part of the land to which the appeal relates, as listed below:

Owner's Name	Address at which the notice was served	Date the notice was served

CERTIFICATES C and D   C & D

If you do not know who owns all or part of the appeal site, complete either Certificate C or Certificate D enclosed with the accompanying Guidance Notes and attach it to the appeal form.

AGRICULTURAL HOLDINGS CERTIFICATE (This has to be completed for all appeals)

We also need to know whether the appeal site forms part of an agricultural holding.
Please tick either (a) or (b).

If the appellant is the <u>sole</u> agricultural tenant, (b) should be ticked and 'not applicable' should be written under 'Tenant's name'.   ✓

a) None of the land to which the appeal relates is, or is part of, an agricultural holding: a

OR

b) The appeal site is, or is part of, an agricultural holding and the appellant (or the agent) has given the requisite notice to every person (other than the appellant) who, on the day 21 days before the date of the appeal, was a tenant of an agricultural holding on all or part of the land to which the appeal relates as listed below: b

Tenant's Name	Address at which the notice was served	Date the notice was served

PLANNING APPLICATION FORMS

J. ESSENTIAL SUPPORTING DOCUMENTS

The documents listed in 1-6 below, <u>must</u> be sent with your appeal form; 7-11 must also be sent if appropriate. If we do not receive <u>all</u> your appeal documents by the end of the 6 month appeal period, we will not deal with it. Please tick the boxes to show which documents you are enclosing.   ✓

1   A copy of the original **planning application** sent to the LPA.   1

2   A copy of the **site ownership certificate and ownership details** submitted to the LPA <u>at application stage</u> (this is usually part of the LPA's planning application form).   2

3   A copy of the **LPA's decision notice** (if issued).   3

4   A **site plan** (preferably on a copy of an Ordnance Survey map at not less than 10,000 scale) showing the general location of the proposed development and its boundary. This plan should show two named roads so as to assist the location of the appeal site or premises. The application site should be edged or shaded in red and any other adjoining land owned or controlled by the appellant (if any) edged or shaded blue.   4

5   A list (stating drawing numbers) and copies of all **plans, drawings and documents** sent to the LPA as part of the application. The plans and drawings should show all boundaries and coloured markings given on those sent to the LPA.   5

6   A list (stating drawing numbers) and copies of any **additional plans, drawings and documents** sent to the LPA but which did not form part of the original application (e.g. drawings for illustrative purposes).   6

Copies of the following must also be sent, if appropriate:

7   **Additional plans, drawings or documents** relating to the application but not previously seen by the LPA. Please number them clearly and list the numbers here: 7

8   Any relevant **correspondence** with the LPA.   8

9   If the appeal is against the LPA's refusal or failure to approve the matters reserved under an outline permission, please enclose:

    (a) the relevant outline application;   9a

    (b) all plans sent at outline application stage;   9b

    (c) the original outline planning permission.   9c

10   If the appeal is against the LPA's refusal or failure to decide an application which relates to a **condition**, we must have a copy of the original permission with the condition attached.   10

11   A copy of any Environmental Statement plus certificates and notices relating to publicity (if one was sent with the application, or required by the LPA).   11

12   If you have sent other appeals for this or nearby sites to us and these have not been decided, please give details and our reference numbers.   12

PLEASE TURN OVER AND SIGN THE FORM - UNSIGNED FORMS WILL BE RETURNED

PLANNING APPLICATION FORMS

K. PLEASE SIGN BELOW

(Signed forms together with all supporting documents must be received by us within the 6 month time limit)

1. I confirm that I have sent a copy of this appeal form and relevant documents to the LPA *(if you do not your appeal will not normally be accepted).*
2. I confirm that all sections have been fully completed and that the details of the ownership (section I) are correct to the best of my knowledge.

Signature   Date

Name (in capitals)

On behalf of (if applicable)

The gathering and subsequent processing of the personal data supplied by you in this form, is in accordance with the terms of our registration under the Data Protection Act 1998. Further information about our Data Protection policy can be found on our website under "Privacy Statement" and in the booklet accompanying this appeal form.

NOW SEND

1 COPY to us at:	1 COPY to the LPA	1 COPY for you to keep
The Planning Inspectorate Registry/Scanning Team Temple Quay House 2 The Square Temple Quay BRISTOL BS1 6PN	Send a copy of the appeal form to the address from which the decision notice was sent (or to the address shown on any letters received from the LPA). There is no need to send them all the documents again, send them any supporting documents not previously sent as part of the application. If you do not send them a copy of this form and documents, we may not accept your appeal.	

When we receive your appeal form, we will:

1. Tell you if it is valid and who is dealing with it.
2. Tell you and the LPA the procedure for your appeal.
3. Tell you the timetable for sending further information or representations.

   YOU MUST KEEP TO THE TIMETABLE
   If information or representations are sent late we may disregard them. They will not be seen by the Inspector but will be sent back to you.
4. Tell you about the arrangements for the site visit, hearing or inquiry.

At the end of the appeal process, the Inspector will give the decision, and the reasons for it, in writing.

Published by The Planning Inspectorate June 2006.

Printed in the UK June 2006 on paper comprising 100% post-consumer waste.

© Crown Copyright 2004. Copyright in the printed material and design is held by the Crown. You can use extracts of this publication in non-commercial in-house material, as long as you show that they came from this document. You should apply in writing if you need to make copies of this document (or any part of it) to:

The Copyright Unit
Her Majesty's Stationery Office
St Clements House
2-6 Colegate
Norwich
NR3 1BQ

PLANNING APPLICATION FORMS

The Planning Inspectorate

Further information about us and the planning appeal system is available on our website
www.planning-inspectorate.gov.uk

For official use only
Date Received

ENFORCEMENT NOTICE APPEAL

If you need this document in large print, on audio tape, in Braille or in another language, please contact our helpline on 0117 372 8075.

Please use a separate form for each appeal against each different enforcement notice.

Before completing this form, please read our booklet 'Making your enforcement appeal' which was sent to you with this form.

Please tick the box if you are also sending this appeal by FAX (details on page 7) ☐

WARNING: The appeal must be received by the Inspectorate before the effective date of the local planning authority's enforcement notice.

PLEASE PRINT CLEARLY IN CAPITALS USING BLACK INK

A. APPELLANT DETAILS

Name

Organisation Name (if applicable)

Address

Postcode

Daytime Tel   Fax

Email

I prefer to be contacted by   Email   Post

B. AGENT DETAILS (if any) FOR THE APPEAL

Name

Organisation Name (if applicable)

Address

Postcode

Your Ref

Daytime Tel   Fax

Email

I prefer to be contacted by   Email   Post

C. LOCAL PLANNING AUTHORITY (LPA) DETAILS

Name of local planning authority (LPA)

Date of issue of enforcement notice   Effective date of enforcement notice

Land affected (please give full address)

Postcode

What is your/the appellant's interest in the land?   owner   occupier   tenant   lessee   licensee

If none of the above, please state your interest

PINS PF03 (REVISED AUGUST 2004)   1   Please turn over

PLANNING APPLICATION FORMS

The Planning Inspectorate - Enforcement Notice Appeal

D. OTHER APPEALS/APPLICATIONS

Have you made any other appeals to the Secretary of State on this, or nearby land, for example, against a refusal of planning permission or of a lawful development certificate.   YES   NO

If yes, please give details, including our reference number if known.

Appeal Ref.

Has the appellant applied for planning permission and paid the appropriate fee for the same development as in the enforcement notice?   YES   NO

IF **YES** PLEASE STATE

a   the date of the relevant application

b   the date of the LPA's decision (if any)

Are there any planning reasons why a fee should not be paid for this appeal?

E. GROUNDS AND FACTS

Please mark ✓ which of the following grounds of appeal apply to your case and give the facts in support of each ground chosen. Refer to our booklet 'Making your enforcement appeal' for help. Please continue on a separate sheet if necessary.

(a) That planning permission should be granted for what is alleged in the notice.

Section 174(2)(a) of the Town and Country Planning Act says "that, in respect of any breach of planning control which may be constituted by the matters stated in the notice, planning permission ought to be granted or, as the case may be, the condition or limitation concerned ought to be discharged".

PLANNING APPLICATION FORMS

(a) (continued)

PLANNING APPLICATION FORMS

(b) That the breach of control alleged in the enforcement notice has not occurred as a matter of fact.

Section 174(2)(b) says "that those matters have not occurred".

(c) That there has not been a breach of planning control (for example because permission has already been granted, or it is permitted development).

Section 174(2)(c) says "that those matters (if they occurred) do not constitute a breach of planning control".

(d) That, at the time the enforcement notice was issued, it was too late to take enforcement action against the matters stated in the notice.

Section 174(2)(d) says "that at the date when the notice was issued, no enforcement action could be taken in respect of any breach of planning control which may be constituted by those matters".

PLANNING APPLICATION FORMS

(e) The notice was not properly served on everyone with an interest in the land.

Section 174(2)(e) says "that copies of the enforcement notice were not served as required by section 172".

(f) The steps required to comply with the requirements of the notice are excessive, and lesser steps would overcome the objections.

Please state how you think the requirements should be varied.

Section 174(2)(f) says "that the steps required by the notice to be taken, or the activities required by the notice to cease, exceed what is necessary to remedy any breach of planning control which may be constituted by those matters or, as the case may be, to remedy any injury to amenity which has been caused by any such breach".

(g) That the time given to comply with the notice is too short.

Please state what you consider to be a reasonable compliance period, and why.

Section 174(2)(g) says "that any period specified in the notice in accordance with section 173(9) falls short of what should reasonably be allowed".

PLANNING APPLICATION FORMS

F. CHOICE OF PROCEDURE

CHOOSE ONE PROCEDURE ONLY

You should start by reading our booklet 'Making your enforcement appeal' which explains the different procedures used to determine enforcement appeals. In short there are 3 possible methods: - written representations, hearings and inquiries. You should consider carefully which method suits your circumstances.

Please note that when we decide how the appeal will proceed we will take into account the LPA's views. ✓

1 WRITTEN REPRESENTATIONS

This is normally the simplest, quickest and most straightforward way of making an appeal. Three out of every four people making an appeal choose this method. The written procedure is particularly suited to small-scale developments (e.g. extensions of buildings, individual houses or small groups of houses, appeals against conditions and changes of use). It is also very popular with people making their own appeal without professional help. The process involves the submission of written 'grounds of appeal' followed by a written statement and any supporting documents. It also provides an opportunity to comment in writing on the Local Planning Authority's reasons for issuing an enforcement notice. An Inspector will study all of the documents before visiting the appeal site/area and issuing a written decision.

NOTE: The Inspector will visit the site <u>unaccompanied</u> by either party unless the relevant part of the site cannot be seen from a road or other public land, or it is essential for the Inspector to enter the site to check measurements or other relevant facts.

a) If the written procedure is agreed, can the relevant part of the appeal site be seen from a road, public footpath, bridleway or other public land?   YES ☐   NO ☐

b) Is it essential for the Inspector to enter the site to check measurements or other relevant facts?   YES ☐   NO ☐

If the answer to **1b** is 'yes' please explain

2 HEARINGS

This process is likely to be suited to slightly more complicated cases which require detailed discussion about the merits of the case. Like the written procedure, the process starts with the submission of 'written grounds of appeal' followed by a full written statement of case and an opportunity to comment in writing on the Local Planning Authority's reasons for issuing an enforcement notice. The Planning Inspectorate will then arrange a hearing at which the Local Planning Authority and the appellant(s) will be represented. Members of the public, interested bodies (e.g. Parish/Town Councils) and the press may also attend. At the hearing the Inspector will lead a discussion on the matters already presented in the written statements and supporting documents. The Inspector will visit the site/area and issue a written decision in the same way as the written procedure.

Although you may prefer a hearing the Inspectorate must consider your appeal suitable for this procedure.

3 INQUIRIES

This is the most formal of procedures. Although it is not a court of law the proceedings will often seem to be quite similar as the parties to the appeal will usually be legally represented and expert witnesses will be called to give evidence. Members of the public and press may also attend. In general, inquiries are suggested for appeals that:

- are complex and particularly controversial;
- have caused a lot of local interest;
- involve the need to question evidence through formal cross-examination.

239

PLANNING APPLICATION FORMS

G. SENDING THE FEE FOR THE DEEMED PLANNING APPLICATION

NOTE: If you intend to plead ground **(a)** and have the deemed planning application considered as part of your appeal **you must pay the fee** shown in the explanatory note accompanying your Enforcement Notice:

The fee to the Planning Inspectorate (made payable to "ODPM") should be sent with your appeal form to the same address: The Planning Inspectorate, PO Box 326, BRISTOL BS99 7XF.

You must also send the fee due to the local planning authority with their copy of the appeal form.

Have you sent the fee for the deemed planning application with this appeal form?   YES   NO

Have you sent the fee to the local planning authority with their copy of the appeal form?   YES   NO

H. CHECK SIGN AND DATE

I have filled in all parts of the form ☐

I have attached a copy of the enforcement notice and plan to this form ☐

I have sent a copy of this form and any documents to the LPA ☐

Signature   Date

Name (in capitals)

On behalf of (if applicable)

The gathering and subsequent processing of the personal data supplied by you in this form, is in accordance with the terms of our registration under the Data Protection Act 1998. Further information about our Data Protection policy can be found on our website under "Privacy Statement" and in the booklet accompanying this appeal form.

NOW SEND

1 COPY to us at:

The Planning Inspectorate
PO Box 326
BRISTOL
BS99 7XF

If you wish to deliver by hand:
(make sure you get a receipt)

The Planning Inspectorate
Customer Support Unit
Temple Quay House
2 The Square
Temple Quay
BRISTOL
BS1 6PN

Fax to: 0117 372 8782

Helpline: ☎ 0117 372 8075

When we receive your appeal form, we will:

1. Tell you if it is valid and who is dealing with it.
2. Tell you and the LPA the procedure for your appeal.
3. Tell you the timetable for sending further information or representations.

    YOU MUST KEEP TO THE TIMETABLE
    If information or representations are sent late we may disregard them. They will not be seen by the Inspector but will be sent back to you.

4. Tell you about the arrangements for the site visit, hearing or inquiry.

At the end of the appeal process, the Inspector will give the decision, and the reasons for it, in writing.

Index

access to neighbouring land 86, 89
access to public information 151–152
advertisement 27–29
 Advertisement Consent 28, 67–70
 Area of Special Control 29
 displaying
  consent not required 67–70
  further considerations 70
 rules 28
 scope of works 67
appeals 10, 122
 decision 136–138
  challenging 137–138
  golden rules 137
 preparation and submission
  information required 126–128
  self-representation 128–129
 process 129
 decision 136–138
 householder appeals service (HAS) 135
 informal hearing 131–133
 length of appeal 135–136
 public inquiry 133–134
 submission of appeal documents 134–135
 written representations 129–131
 processing 122–126
approvals see consents or approvals
Area of Outstanding Natural Beauty (AONB) 26
Area of Special Control of Advertisements 29

Breach of Condition Notice 141
Broads 26–27
Building Regulations 77–78, 88

241

INDEX

development process 89–90
  approved works changed during construction 90–91
  completion of works 9
buildings of architectural interest *see* listed building
bungalows *see* dwelling

Certificate of Lawful Use or Development 143
Certificate of Proposed Lawful Development or Use 73
  application 73–76
  checklist 76–77
  approved works changed during construction 90–92
chimneys
  installation
    planning permission not required 58
    scope of works 58
consents or approvals 35
  access to neighbouring land 86, 89
  Advertisement Consent 28
  Building Regulations 77–78, 88
    checklist 35–41, 88–89
  Conservation Area Consent 85, 88
  Listed Building Consent 21–22, 83–85, 88

party walls 78–79, 88
planning conditions 80–81, 88
Restrictive Covenants 81–83, 88
Rights to Light 85–86, 89
Scheduled Ancient Monument Consent 24
Tree Preservation Order (TPO) 87, 89
wildlife 86–87, 89
conservation area 22–24
  article 1(5) land 26
  Conservation Area Consent 85, 88
curtilage of dwelling 18–19
  providing off street parking, driveways and hardstandings
    planning permission not required 67
    scope of works 67

demolition of any building or structure
  further considerations 61
  planning permission not required 60–61
  scope of works 60
Design and Access Statements 9, 102
development 12–13
  definition 12–13
  key test 5

INDEX

permitted development 13–14
  approved works changed during construction 90–92
  original building 13–14
Permitted Development rights 6, 14
  article 1(5) land 26
  confirmation requests 73
  conservation area 23
  curtilage of dwelling 19
  dwellings 17
  highway 20–21
  Use Classes 20
development plan 14–16
development process 89–90
  completion of works 90
  approved works changed during construction 90–92
dimensions *see* measurements
discharging conditions 117
drawings
  appropriate scale 45
  specific requirements 45
driveways
  within curtilage of home
    planning permission not required 67
    scope of works 67
dwelling 16–18
  curtilage 18–19

display of advertisement
  Advertisement Consent not required 67–70
  further considerations 70
  scope of works 67
further considerations
  adding solar panels and microgeneration equipment or to building in garden 55
  demolition of any building or structure 61
  display of advertisement 70
  enlargement by altering shape of roof 52–53
  enlargement, improvement or alteration 48
  installation of microwave antenna on house or within garden 60
  painting 58
  subdividing or changing use of home 57
  working from home 56
  meaning 2–4, 16–17
planning permission not required
  adding a porch 50

243

INDEX

adding solar panels and microgeneration equipment or to building in garden 54
altering roof without changing shape 51
demolition of any building or structure 60–61
enlargement by altering shape of roof 52
enlargement, improvement or alteration 47–50
installation of chimneys, flues, soil and vent pipes 58
installation of microwave antenna on house or within garden 59
painting 58
subdividing or changing use of home 57
working from home 56
'purposes incidental' to enjoyment 19–20
scope of works
  adding a porch 50
  adding solar panels and microgeneration equipment or to building in garden 54
  altering roof without changing shape 51
  demolition of any building or structure 60

display of advertisement 67
enlargement by altering shape of roof 52
enlargement, improvement or alteration 47
installation of chimneys, flues, soil and vent pipes 58
installation of microwave antenna on house or within garden 59
painting 58
subdividing or changing use of home 57
working from home 56
dwellinghouse
  meaning 2–4, 16–17

Enforcement Notice 140
England
  National Park Authorities 26–27, 190–191
  planning authorities 155–184
Environmental Impact Assessment (EIA) 29–31, 102–103

fences see gates, walls and fences
flues
  installation
    planning permission not required 58
    scope of works 58

INDEX

Freedom of Information Act 2000 151
fuel tank or container
  erecting in garden
    further considerations 72
    planning permission not required 72
    scope of works 71

garden
  constructing shed, summerhouse, greenhouse, swimming pool or other enclosure
    further assistance 66
    further considerations 65
    planning permission not required 64–65
    scope of works 64
    useful definitions 65
  creating new vehicular access
    planning permission not required 66
    planning permission required 66
    scope of works 66
  display of advertisement
    Advertisement Consent not required 67–70
    further considerations 70
    scope of works 67
  further considerations
    constructing shed, summerhouse, greenhouse, swimming pool or other enclosure 65
    display of advertisement 70
    erecting fuel tank or container 72
    erecting gates, walls and fences 62–63
    installing standalone solar panel 71
    planting hedges and trees 64
  planning permission not required
    constructing shed, summerhouse, greenhouse, swimming pool or other enclosure 64–65
    creating new vehicular access 66
    erecting fuel tank or container 72
    erecting gates, walls and fences 62
    installing standalone solar panel 71
    planting hedges and trees 63
    providing off street parking, driveways and hardstandings within curtilage of home 67

INDEX

Permitted Development
    rights 6, 14
  article 1(5) land 26
  confirmation requests 73
  conservation area 23
  curtilage of dwelling 19
  dwellings 17
  highway 20–21
  Use Classes 20
Planning Act 2008 4, 5
Planning and
    Compensation Act
  1991 4
Planning and Compulsory
    Purchase Act 2004
  4
  s. 38(6) 5
planning applications
    93–94
  checklist of information
    required
    full planning application
      98–101
    outline planning
      application 95–98
  decision-making process
    108–111
    section 106
      agreements
      111–113
    withdrawal of
      application 113
  eligibility 32
  forms 207–240
  golden rules 114
  pre-application
    discussions
    with neighbours 95
    with council 94–95
  refusal
    appeal *see* appeals
    reapplication 121–122
  submission 101–102
    assistance with
      103–105
    councils' powers to
      decline applications
      101–102
    Design and Access
      Statements 102
    Environmental Impact
      Assessment
      102–103
    online 105
    processing of
      application
      106–108
planning authorities
  England 155–184
  Greater London
    184–187
  Wales 188–190
planning conditions
  80–81, 88,
  115–117
Planning Contravention
    Notice 140
planning decision 114
  challenging 118–119
  discharging conditions
    117
  planning conditions
    115–117
Planning (Listed Buildings
    and Conservation
    Areas) Act 1990 4

INDEX

planning permission
  applications *see* planning applications
  decision *see* planning decision
  implementation 117–118
    amendments to approved drawings 118
    challenging planning decision 118–119
    final checks 119–120
    golden rules 120
  not required
    Certificate of Proposed Lawful Development or Use *see* Certificate of Proposed Lawful Development or Use
    confirmation from council 73
    consents or approvals required before proceeding with work *see* consents or approvals
    development process 89–90
    dwellings and gardens *see* dwelling; garden
  starting work without permission *see* unauthorised developments
Planning Policy Statements (PPSs) 8–9
planning regulations 6
article 1(5) land 26–27
planning system 4
  Design and Access Statements 9
  key facts 11
  key planning acts 4–5
  key test for all development 5
  Local Development Frameworks (LDFs) 7, 8
  Local Development Plans 6–7
  national planning policy guidance 8–9
  Permitted Development rights 6
  Planning Policy Statements (PPSs) 8–9
  Regional Policy Guidance notes (RPGs) 7, 8–9
  Regional Spatial Strategies (RSSs) 7
  right of appeal 10
  structure 9–10
  summary 11
professional assistance 33–34
public inquiry 133–134

Regional Policy Guidance notes (RPGs) 7
Regional Spatial Strategies (RSSs) 7
Restrictive Covenants 81–83, 88

INDEX

Rights to Light 85–86, 88

Scheduled Ancient Monument 24
Scheduled Ancient Monument Consent 24
Scotland 32–33
　National Parks 26–27
Screening Opinion 30
　application 103
shed
　constructing in garden
　　further assistance 66
　　further considerations 65
　　planning permission not required 64–65
　　scope of works 64
　　useful definitions 65
soil and vent pipes
　installation
　　planning permission not required 58
　　scope of works 58
solar panels and microgeneration equipment
　further considerations
　　adding to home or to building in garden 55
　　installing standalone panel in garden 71

planning permission not required
　adding to home or to building in garden 54
　installing standalone panel in garden 71
scope of works
　adding to home or to building in garden 54
　installing standalone panel in garden 71
sources of useful information 192–194
South Downs 27
Stop Notice 140
summerhouse
　constructing in garden
　　further assistance 66
　　further considerations 65
　　planning permission not required 64–65
　　scope of works 64
　　useful definitions 65
Sunday Times
　top ten tips for adding value to home 1
swimming pool
　constructing in garden
　　further assistance 66
　　further considerations 65
　　planning permission not required 64–65
　　scope of works 64
　　useful definitions 65

250

INDEX

technical assistance 33–34
Temporary Stop Notice 140–141
Town and Country Planning Act 1990 4–5
Town and Country Planning (General Permitted Development) Order 1995 (SI 1995/418) 6
Town and Country Planning (General Permitted Development) (Amendment) Order 1998 (SI 1998/462) 6
Town and Country Planning (General Permitted Development) (Amendment) (England) Order 2008 (SI 2008/675) 6
Town and Country Planning (General Permitted Development) (Amendment) (No. 2) (England) Order 2008 (SI 2008/2362) 6
Tree Preservation Order (TPO) 31–32, 87, 89

trees
  planting in garden
    further considerations 64
    planning permission not required 63
    scope of works 63

unauthorised developments 139, 142–143
  buildings of architectural interest 141–142
  Certificate of Lawful Use 143
  enforcement tools 140
    Breach of Condition Notice 141
    Enforcement Notice 140
    Planning Contravention Notice 140
    Stop Notice 140
    Temporary Stop Notice 140–141
  impact on neighbours 142
Unitary Development Plans (UDPs) 7, 16
Use Classes 20
vehicular access
  planning permission not required 66
  planning permission required 66
  scope of works 66

Wales 32–33
  National Park Authorities 26–27, 190–191

INDEX

planning authorities 188–190
walls *see* gates, walls and fences; party walls
wildlife 86–87, 89
Wildlife and Countryside Act 1981, s. 41(3) 26

working from home
 further considerations 56
 planning permission not required 56
 scope of works 56
World Heritage site 26–27
written representations 129–131